Precious BLOOD OF JESUS Novena

Augustine Teresa

A 9-Day Journey to Deepen Your Devotion and Experience Divine Mercy | Drenching Yourself in the Mercy of God

Copyright©2024 Augustine Teresa All right reserved

The following content is for informational purposes only. It is presented based on general religious understanding and may vary depending on specific denominations or interpretations. Please refer to your religious leader or trusted resources for guidance on matters of faith and practice.

Unauthorized reproduction, alteration, or distribution of any part of this publication by means of duplication, recording, or any electronic or mechanical methods is strictly prohibited without prior approval from the publisher. However, limited excerpts may be used for critical analysis and specific non-commercial purposes in accordance with copyright regulations, exempt from the aforementioned prohibition.

Table of Content

Introduction...8
   How to Use This Book..10
   A Historical Context: The Power of the Precious Blood in Christian Tradition...13
   Understanding the Novena: Structure and Purpose............19
      Purpose of a Novena:.. 20
   Preparing for Your Novena: Embracing the Precious Blood 23

Day 1: The Blood of the Covenant - Unveiling the Profound Gift..27
   Scripture Readings: Exploring the Significance of Blood in Salvation History... 27
   Reflecting on the Sacrifice and Covenant Established by Christ's Blood.. 36
   Day 1 – Novena to the Precious Blood of Jesus................... 40
   Daily Reflection Prompts: Day 1 - The Blood of the Covenant..42
   Intercessory Prayer: Petitions for Forgiveness and Renewal. 45

Day 2: Blood of Strength and Courage - Finding Fortitude in Christ.. 49
   Exploring the Theme: Strength for Martyrs, Saints, and Everyday Believers.. 49
   Readings and Reflections - Examples of Strength Inspired by Christ's Blood.. 53

Day 2 – Novena to the Precious Blood of Jesus..................58

Daily Prayer: Seeking Courage for Challenges and Spiritual Growth..60

Reflective Journaling: Identifying Areas Where You Need Strength...62

Litany of the Precious Blood.................................66

Day 3: Blood of Cleansing and Purification - Embracing the Power of Redemption..69

Scriptural Basis: The Blood as Cleansing Agent and Washing Away of Sins..69

Guided Meditation: Visualizing Purification Through Christ's Sacrifice...73

Day 3 – Novena to the Precious Blood of Jesus..................77

Prayer for Forgiveness and Renewal......................................79

Self-Examination Prompts: Acknowledging Areas for Growth..82

Act of Consecration to the Precious Blood..........................86

Day 4: Blood of Unity and Reconciliation - Healing Brokenness and Building Bridges..93

Theme Exploration: The Blood as a Unifying Force, Mending Divisions..93

Scriptural Examples: Passages Highlighting Reconciliation Through Christ..97

Day 4 – Novena to the Precious Blood of Jesus.................100
    Daily Prayer for Peace and Healing in Relationships.......... 102
    Journaling Prompt: Identifying Broken Relationships...... 104
    Intercessory Prayer for Reconciliation in the Wider World 108

Day 5: Blood of Compassion and Healing - Experiencing Divine Mercy..111
    Examining the Theme: The Blood as a Source of God's Unconditional Love and Healing... 111
    Readings and Reflections: Miracles and Healing Through Christ's Blood... 115

Day 5 – Novena to the Precious Blood of Jesus.................119
    Guided Visualization: Experiencing God's Healing Love.. 122
    Prayer for Those in Need of Healing................................... 126

Day 6: Blood of Hope and New Life - Finding Transformation and Strength.. 129
    Scriptural Exploration: The Blood as a Symbol of Resurrection and New Beginnings.. 129

Day 6 – Novena to the Precious Blood of Jesus.................133
    Daily Prayer for Hope and Transformation........................ 135
    Reflective Journaling: Identifying Areas for Personal Transformation..137
    Meditation on the Power of the Blood to Grant New Life 141
    Intercessory Prayer for Those Struggling with Loss or Despair

Day 7: Blood of Light and Illumination - Finding Clarity and Direction.. 147

Examining the Theme: The Blood as a Source of Spiritual Light and Guidance..147

Prayer for Clarity and Direction:...151

Readings and Reflections: Passages Where Christ Offers Guidance and Wisdom...152

Day 7 – Novena to the Precious Blood of Jesus..................156

Prayer for Discernment and Clarity.......................................158

Journaling Prompt: Identifying Areas Where You Seek Direction..159

Day 8: Blood of Intercession and Advocacy - Finding Strength in Prayer.. 167

Understanding the Power of Intercessory Prayer.................167

Scriptural Examples: Christ's Intercession for Humanity.. 171

Day 8 – Novena to the Precious Blood of Jesus...................174

Prayer for the Needs of the Church and the World............176

Chaplet of the Precious Blood..178

Intercessory Prayer for Specific Needs..................................180

Day 9: Blood of Eternal Life - Gratitude and Looking Forward... 185

Scripture Readings: Focus on Eternal Life Promised Through

Christ's Sacrifice.. 185
    Deepening Your Exploration.. 188
Day 9 – Novena to the Precious Blood of Jesus................... 189
Closing Prayer of the Novena: Expressing Gratitude and Continued Commitment..191
Reflective Journaling: Reflecting on Your Novena Experience and Commitments Moving Forward...................193
Litany of Thanksgiving to the Precious Blood................... 196
Appendix.. 201
Additional Prayers and Devotions Associated with the Precious Blood... 202

Introduction

Welcome, dear reader, to a transformative journey of nine days. We invite you to embark on a pilgrimage of faith, a **novena** dedicated to the profound mystery of the Precious Blood of Jesus Christ.

This novena is more than just a set of prayers; it's an invitation to delve deeper into the heart of God's redemptive love. Over the next nine days, we will explore the immense significance of Christ's sacrifice, allowing His Precious Blood to wash over us, cleansing, healing, and renewing our spirits.

As we embark on this sacred journey, imagine yourselves setting out on a pilgrimage, each day a step closer to a deeper understanding of God's grace. We will encounter scripture passages that illuminate the power of the Precious Blood, reflections that prompt contemplation, and prayers that express our gratitude and yearning for transformation.

This novena is open to all who seek a closer relationship with Jesus Christ. Whether you are a seasoned believer or just beginning to explore your faith, the message of the Precious Blood holds immense power to transform your life.

So, prepare your hearts and minds for a profound encounter. Let us open ourselves to the transformative power of Christ's sacrifice and allow His Precious Blood to guide us on this enriching pilgrimage of faith.

How to Use This Book

This novena is designed to be a personal and transformative experience spread over nine days. Here's a guide to help you navigate your journey:

Daily Structure: Each day of the novena follows a similar structure, providing a framework for focused reflection and prayer.

Opening Prayer: Begin each day with the provided opening prayer, setting the intention for your meditation and aligning your heart with God's will.

Scripture: Reflect on the designated scripture passage for the day. Consider its meaning, how it relates to the theme of the Precious Blood, and how it applies to your life.

Meditation: Each day offers a unique meditation prompt. Take some quiet time to ponder the questions or themes presented. Journaling your reflections can deepen your understanding.

Prayer: A heartfelt prayer specifically tailored to the day's theme is included. Feel free to personalize it by adding your own petitions and expressions of gratitude.

Closing Reflection: Conclude each day with a brief reflection to solidify the day's message in your mind and heart.

Daily Commitment: Consider incorporating a small, concrete action into your day that reflects the theme you explored. This could be a prayer practice, an act of service, or a period of focused gratitude.

Additional Tips:

Find a Quiet Space: Dedicate a specific time and place each day for your novena prayers and reflections. Minimize distractions to create a sacred space for focused contemplation.

Be Open-Minded: Approach the novena with an open heart and a willingness to learn and grow.

Journaling: Keeping a journal throughout the novena can be a valuable tool. Use it to capture your reflections, insights, and prayers.

Community: Share your experience with others! Discuss the novena with friends, family, or a faith group. Sharing your journey can deepen your understanding and provide support.

Remember, this novena is a personal journey. Adapt the pace and approach to suit your needs and preferences. The most important thing is to open yourself to the transformative power of the Precious Blood and allow it to enrich your life.

A Historical Context: The Power of the Precious Blood in Christian Tradition

The concept of blood holding immense significance has been present throughout human history, often seen as a carrier of life force and a symbol of sacrifice. Within Christianity, the blood of Jesus Christ, referred to as the Precious Blood, takes on a central and deeply meaningful role. To fully appreciate the power of the Precious Blood in Christian tradition, we must delve into its historical development and theological underpinnings.

Early Church and the Blood as Covenant

The roots of the devotion to the Precious Blood can be traced back to the very foundation of Christianity. The Hebrew Bible establishes the concept of blood as a vital element in God's covenant with the Israelites. In **Exodus 24:6-8,** Moses sprinkled the blood of sacrificed animals on the altar and the people, signifying a binding agreement between God and his chosen people. Early Christians saw Jesus' sacrifice as the ultimate fulfillment of these Old Testament covenants, with His blood sealing a new and everlasting covenant between God and humanity **(Hebrews 9:11-15).**

The Power of Redemption

The shedding of Christ's blood is not merely symbolic; it represents the act of redemption for humankind. Sin, according to Christian belief, separates humanity from God. Passages like **Romans 3:23** state, "for all have sinned and fall short of the glory of God," emphasizing the universality of sin. The early Church Fathers, such as Irenaeus, saw Jesus' blood as the necessary price to pay for humanity's sin. His sacrifice, through the shedding of His blood, offers forgiveness, reconciliation, and the potential for eternal life **(1 John 1:7).**

Development of Devotion and Artistic Expression

While the significance of Christ's blood was acknowledged from the beginning, a specific devotion to the Precious Blood emerged around the 12th and 13th centuries. Saint Bernard of Clairvaux, a highly influential figure, is credited with promoting this devotion through his writings and sermons, emphasizing the immense love demonstrated by Christ's sacrifice.

This period also saw a flourishing of artistic expression depicting the Precious Blood. Images of the Crucifixion often highlighted the wounds on Jesus' body, from which blood flowed freely. Additionally, the **"Fountain of Life"** imagery emerged, portraying Christ as the source of life-giving blood pouring forth to nourish humanity. These artistic representations served as powerful visual reminders of the redemptive power of the Precious Blood.

Mystical Experiences and Eucharistic Connection

Mystical experiences of certain saints further fueled the devotion to the Precious Blood. Saint Gertrude the Great and Saint Catherine of Siena, for example, reported visions that emphasized the transformative power of Christ's blood. These experiences resonated with the faithful, deepening their understanding of the Precious Blood's significance.

The concept of the Precious Blood is intricately linked with the Eucharist, the central sacrament of the Catholic Church. Catholics believe that during the consecration of bread and wine, a transformation (transubstantiation) occurs, making them the actual body and blood of Christ. Receiving the Eucharist, then, becomes a way to partake in the sacrifice of Christ and receive the benefits of His Precious Blood.

Challenges and Reforms

The devotion to the Precious Blood faced some challenges during the Reformation period. Protestant reformers like Martin Luther downplayed the role of veneration of physical elements like relics or the Eucharist, focusing more on faith alone for salvation. However, the core belief in the redemptive power of Christ's sacrifice remained central to Christian faith across denominations.

The Feast of the Precious Blood

The devotion to the Precious Blood received official recognition within the Catholic Church with the establishment of the Feast of the Precious Blood in 1849 by Pope Pius IX. This feast, celebrated on July 1st, serves as a dedicated day to reflect on the profound meaning of Christ's sacrifice.

Enduring Legacy

Today, the devotion to the Precious Blood continues to hold significance for many Christians. It serves as a powerful reminder of God's boundless love, the sacrifice made for humanity's redemption, and the ongoing presence of Christ's grace through the Eucharist. Whether through prayer, meditation, or artistic expression, the Precious Blood remains a potent symbol that continues to inspire and transform the lives of believers.

Further Exploration:

For a deeper dive into the theology of the Precious Blood, consider studying the writings of Church Fathers like Saint Irenaeus or Saint Augustine.

Explore devotional practices related to the Precious Blood, such as novenas, prayers, or hymns.

Many churches possess artwork depicting the Precious Blood. Visiting these can provide a visual connection to the devotion's historical and artistic expressions.

Understanding the Novena: Structure and Purpose

The novena you're embarking on is a specific devotional practice within Christianity, offering a structured approach to prayer and reflection over nine consecutive days. Understanding the novena's structure and purpose will help you get the most out of this spiritual journey.

Structure of a Novena:

A traditional novena follows a similar format each day:

Opening Prayer: This sets the intention for the day's reflection and aligns your heart with God's will.

Scripture: A designated scripture passage related to the novena's theme is presented for reflection. Consider its meaning and how it applies to your life.

Meditation: Each day offers a prompt or theme for focused contemplation. Journaling your thoughts and feelings can deepen your understanding.

Prayer: A specific prayer tailored to the day's theme is provided. Feel free to personalize it by adding your own petitions and expressions of gratitude.

Closing Reflection: Conclude each day with a brief reflection to solidify the message in your mind and heart.

Purpose of a Novena:

Novenas serve several purposes:

Deepen Faith: By focusing on a specific theme or devotion for nine days, a novena allows for a deeper exploration of its meaning and significance.

Focused Prayer: The structure of a novena provides a framework for consistent prayer and reflection, fostering a sense of discipline and commitment.

Intercession: Novenas can be used to petition God for specific graces or intentions.

Preparation: Sometimes novenas are used as a period of preparation for a feast day or a significant event in the Church calendar.

Spiritual Growth: Through prayer, reflection, and meditation, novenas can be a catalyst for personal growth and a renewed connection with God.

The Novena Dedicated to the Precious Blood:

The novena you're undertaking specifically focuses on the Precious Blood of Jesus Christ. Over the next nine days, you'll explore various aspects of this powerful symbol in Christian faith. The themes may include:

- The concept of blood as a covenant and sacrifice.
- The redemptive power of Christ's blood.
- The connection between the Precious Blood and the Eucharist.
- The ongoing presence of Christ's grace through His sacrifice.

By reflecting on these themes through daily prayers and meditations, this novena aims to deepen your understanding of the Precious Blood's significance and allow you to experience its transformative power in your life.

Preparing for Your Novena: Embracing the Precious Blood

As you embark on this nine-day pilgrimage of faith dedicated to the Precious Blood of Jesus, here are some steps to prepare your heart and mind for a truly enriching experience:

Set an Intention:

Reflect on what you hope to gain from this novena. Do you seek deeper understanding, healing, a renewed sense of faith, or perhaps a specific grace? Having a clear intention will guide your prayers and meditations throughout the journey.

Create a Sacred Space:

Dedicate a specific time and place for your daily novena prayers and reflections. This could be a quiet corner in your home, a church pew, or a peaceful outdoor space. Minimize distractions by silencing your phone and creating an atmosphere conducive to focused contemplation.

Gather Necessary Materials:

You'll likely need a copy of this novena book, a Bible for the designated scripture readings, and a journal for capturing your reflections and prayers. Having a small candle (optional) to light during your prayer time can add a touch of serenity.

Prepare Your Heart:

Take some time for introspection before beginning the novena. Confession (if you practice a denomination that offers it) can be a way to clear your conscience and approach the novena with a sense of openness and receptivity.

Forgive yourself and others. Holding onto resentment can hinder your spiritual growth.

Open Yourself to Transformation:

Approach the novena with a willingness to learn and grow. Be open to the messages that may emerge through scripture, meditations, and prayers. Allow the Precious Blood to wash over you, cleansing and renewing your spirit.

Additional Tips:

Share Your Journey: Consider participating in the novena with a friend or family member. Sharing your experiences and insights can deepen your understanding and provide mutual support.

Seek Inspiration: Explore devotional resources related to the Precious Blood, such as hymns, artwork, or writings of saints.

Maintain Focus: Life can get busy. Set reminders to ensure you dedicate time each day for your novena prayers and reflections.

By following these steps and approaching the novena with an open heart, you'll be well-prepared to embark on this

26

transformative journey of faith, guided by the power of the Precious Blood of Jesus Christ.

Day 1: The Blood of the Covenant - Unveiling the Profound Gift

Scripture Readings: Exploring the Significance of Blood in Salvation History

The concept of blood plays a profound role throughout the Bible, symbolizing life, sacrifice, and ultimately, redemption through Jesus Christ. This novena will delve into key scripture passages that illuminate the significance of blood in salvation history.

Day 1: Genesis 9:3-5

Passage: *"Every moving thing that lives shall be food for you. And as I gave you the green plants, I give you everything. But you must not eat flesh with its lifeblood in it, for the life of the creature is in the blood, and I have given it to you on the* *altar to make atonement for yourselves. It is the blood that makes atonement for one's life."* (Genesis 9:3-5)

Significance: Even in the aftermath of the flood, God establishes a principle regarding blood. Blood is recognized as carrying the life force of a creature. This passage lays the groundwork for the understanding of blood as a vital element in sacrificial offerings.

Day 2: Exodus 12:1-14

Passage: This passage details the instructions for the Passover meal, commemorating the Israelites' liberation from Egypt. The blood of a sacrificed lamb is smeared on the doorposts, marking the homes for protection from the Angel of Death.

Significance: The blood of the lamb becomes a symbol of deliverance and salvation. It foreshadows the ultimate sacrifice of Jesus

Christ, the "**Lamb of God**" who takes away the sin of the world **(John 1:29)**.

Day 3: Leviticus 17:11

Passage: "For the life of the flesh is in the blood, and I have given it to you on the altar to make atonement for yourselves. It is the blood that makes atonement for one's life." **(Leviticus 17:11)**

Significance: This passage in Leviticus reiterates the concept of blood being linked to atonement and forgiveness. The sacrificial system prescribed specific offerings involving the blood of animals, representing a temporary covering of sins.

Day 4: Isaiah 53:5-6

Passage: "But he was wounded for our transgressions, he was bruised for our iniquities; the chastisement for our peace was upon him, and by his stripes we are healed. All we like sheep have gone astray; we have turned every one to his own way; and the Lord has laid on him the iniquity of us all." (Isaiah 53:5-6)

Significance: This powerful passage from Isaiah, often referred to as the "suffering servant" prophecy, foreshadows the sacrifice of Jesus Christ. The text speaks of his wounds and the healing that comes through his suffering.

Day 5: Hebrews 9:11-15

Passage: "When Christ came as high priest of the good things to come, he entered through the greater and more perfect tabernacle, not made with hands, that is, not of this creation. Nor was it with the blood of goats and calves, but with his own blood he entered once for all into the holy places, having obtained eternal redemption. For since the Law possesses only a shadow of the good things to come—not the true form of these realities—how can it, by the same sacrifices that are continually offered every year, make perfect those who approach? Otherwise, would they not have ceased to be offered, since the worshipers, having been cleansed once, would have no longer any consciousness of sins? But in these sacrifices there is a reminder of sins every year. For it is impossible for the blood of bulls and goats to take away sins." (Hebrews 9:11-15)

Significance: The book of Hebrews contrasts the temporary sacrifices of the Old Testament with the ultimate sacrifice of Jesus Christ. His blood, shed once and for all, offers eternal redemption, surpassing the limitations of the animal sacrifices.

Day 6 to Day 9:

Here are daily reflection prompts to guide you through the remaining days of your novena dedicated to the Precious Blood of Jesus Christ:

Day 6: The Precious Blood and the Eucharist

Scripture Reading: (Consider Matthew 26:26-28 or 1 Corinthians 11:23-25)

Reflection Prompts:

- How does the concept of the Eucharist connect to the Precious Blood?

- When you receive the Eucharist, how do you approach it? Is it simply a ritual, or a way to connect with Christ's sacrifice?

- How can you deepen your appreciation for the Eucharist in your daily life?

Day 7: Healing Through the Precious Blood

Scripture Reading: (Consider Isaiah 53:5 or 1 Peter 2:24)

Reflection Prompts:

- Think of a time when you felt wounded or broken. How can Christ's sacrifice offer healing for your emotional or spiritual wounds?

- Consider areas in your life where you need forgiveness, either from yourself or others. How can the Precious Blood facilitate this process?

•Reflect on ways you can extend healing and forgiveness to those who have hurt you.

Day 8: The Power of the Precious Blood in Our Lives

Scripture Reading: (Consider Romans 5:1-5 or Ephesians 2:13-18)

Reflection Prompts:

•How does the concept of the Precious Blood bring you hope or strength?

•In what ways do you experience the ongoing power of Christ's sacrifice in your daily life?

•Think of a personal challenge you're facing. How can the Precious Blood empower you to overcome it?

Day 9: A Life Transformed by the Precious Blood

Scripture Reading: (Consider John 15:1-17 or Philippians 4:13)

Reflection Prompts:

- As you conclude this novena, how has your understanding of the Precious Blood deepened?

- In what ways do you feel transformed by this experience?

- How can you carry the message of the Precious Blood into your daily life and relationships?

Additional Tips:

- Feel free to adapt these prompts to your own personal experiences and reflections.

- Use your journal to capture your thoughts, feelings, and any insights that emerge throughout the novena.

•Sharing your reflections with a trusted friend or family member can deepen your understanding and provide support.

By engaging with these daily prompts and allowing yourself to be guided by the spirit, you can cultivate a deeper connection to the transformative power of the Precious Blood of Jesus Christ.

Additional Exploration:

These are just a few key scripture passages that highlight the significance of blood in salvation history. For further exploration, consider reading:

Exodus 24:6-8 (Covenant established through blood)

Romans 3:23 (Universality of sin)

1 John 1:7 (Cleansing power of Christ's blood)

Revelation 1:5 (Jesus referred to as the "Lamb who was slain")

By meditating on these scriptures and their connection to the Precious Blood of Jesus Christ, you can deepen

Reflecting on the Sacrifice and Covenant Established by Christ's Blood

Finding a Quiet Space:

Begin by creating a sacred space for your meditation. Find a quiet corner, perhaps light a candle, and silence any distractions. Take a few deep breaths to center yourself and open your heart to reflection.

Contemplating the Sacrifice:

• Recall the scripture passages you read about the Passover lamb and the sacrificial system.

• Imagine the scene of Jesus in the Garden of Gethsemane, the emotional and physical anguish he endured.

- Consider the act of crucifixion, the shedding of his blood.

Questions for Reflection:

- How does contemplating Jesus' sacrifice make you feel? Awe, sorrow, gratitude?
- Can you relate his suffering to challenges you've faced in your own life?

The New Covenant:

- Reflect on the concept of a covenant. Think of a promise made between two people, sealed with a handshake or perhaps a signed agreement.
- How does the shedding of Christ's blood establish a new covenant between God and humanity?

Covenant and Commitment:

- A covenant implies a two-way street. God offers forgiveness, grace, and the promise of salvation through Christ's sacrifice. What is your response to this gift?

- Consider areas in your life where you might need to forgive yourself or others.

- How can you live a life that reflects the values of the new covenant – love, compassion, service to others?

Journaling:

- Take some time to journal your reflections. Write down your thoughts, feelings, and any insights that may have emerged during your meditation.

Closing Prayer:

Conclude your meditation with a prayer expressing your gratitude for Christ's sacrifice and your commitment to living a life worthy of the new covenant.

Here's a sample prayer you can adapt:

Dear Lord,

As I reflect on the immense sacrifice you made for me, my heart overflows with gratitude. Your love is beyond comprehension.

I open myself to the grace of the new covenant established by your precious blood. Help me to forgive myself and others, and to live a life that reflects your teachings.

Amen.

Remember, there are no right or wrong answers in meditation. Allow yourself to be guided by the spirit and trust that these

reflections will lead you to a deeper understanding of Christ's sacrifice and the transformative power of the Precious Blood.

Day 1 – Novena to the Precious Blood of Jesus

Let us begin in the name of the Father, and of the Son, and of the Holy Spirit. Amen.

By the power of Thy Blood, O Jesus, I seek Thy aid and implore Thy assistance in this time of need.

O Jesus, I kneel at Thy bleeding feet, pleading for Thy attention. Many graces and mercies have been granted through Thy Blood. My hope remains steadfast in You until the end of my days.

O Jesus, through the Precious Blood shed for our souls, each drop spilled for our redemption, and the tears of Thy Immaculate Mother, I earnestly beseech Thee to hear my prayer:

(Mention your request here…)

O Jesus, throughout Thy mortal life, You consoled countless sufferers, healed numerous infirmities, and often uplifted the downtrodden; have mercy on my soul as it cries to Thee from the depths of anguish.

O Jesus, from the wounds of Thy heart, may a wave of Thy merciful Blood flow forth, granting me the grace I ardently desire.

O Jesus, hasten the moment when my tears will be transformed into joy and my sighs into thanksgivings.

Holy Mary, I ask for your intercession in seeking this aid. But above all, God our Father in heaven, "May Your will be done." Amen.

Recite: Our Father... Hail Mary... Glory Be...

Jesus, Crucified, Have Mercy on Me

Daily Reflection Prompts: Day 1 - The Blood of the Covenant

Building on the Scripture:

Today's scripture passage from Genesis 9:3-5 establishes a principle regarding blood. Reflect on the concept of blood as the life force and its connection to sacrifice in this passage.

Reflection Questions:

•In your own understanding, why might blood be seen as such a powerful symbol?

•Consider how the idea of blood being linked to life connects to the concept of sacrifice. What is being given up, and what life is it potentially sustaining?

- How does this concept from the Old Testament foreshadow the significance of Jesus' sacrifice in the New Testament?

Connecting to Your Life:

- Think of a time when you made a significant sacrifice for someone or something you cared about. How did it make you feel?

- Reflect on areas in your life where you might be hesitant to make a sacrifice. Is there something holding you back?

- Consider the concept of a "covenant" – a binding agreement. How does the idea of a covenant established through blood add a deeper meaning to the relationship between God and humanity?

Prayer and Intention Setting:

- As you begin this novena, what is your intention? What do you hope to gain from a deeper exploration of the Precious Blood?

•Conclude your reflection with a prayer expressing your openness to learning and transformation. Here's a sample prayer you can adapt:

Dear God,

As I embark on this novena dedicated to the Precious Blood, I open my heart to learn and grow in my understanding. Help me to see the connections between the Old and New Testaments, and how the sacrifice of your Son offers new life and hope.

Amen.

Remember: There are no right or wrong answers. Approach these prompts with an open mind and allow the spirit to guide your reflections. Journaling your thoughts and

feelings can be a valuable tool throughout this novena.

Intercessory Prayer: Petitions for Forgiveness and Renewal

Almighty God,

As we gather at the foot of the cross, reflecting on the immense sacrifice of your Son, Jesus Christ, we come before you with hearts filled with humility and longing. Through the shedding of His Precious Blood, a new and everlasting covenant of forgiveness and grace was established.

Petitions for Forgiveness:

We confess our shortcomings, Lord. The times we have strayed from your path, the choices that caused pain to ourselves and others. Wash away our sins with the cleansing power of Christ's blood.

We forgive those who have trespassed against us, and we ask for the strength to release resentment and anger. May your love guide us towards reconciliation and healing.

Petitions for Renewal:

Renew our spirits, O Lord. Fill us with your love and compassion. Grant us the courage to turn away from temptation and embrace a life that reflects your teachings.

We pray for the strength to overcome challenges and to persevere through trials. May the power of the Precious Blood guide us and give us hope.

Intercessions:

We lift up those who are suffering, Lord. The sick, the lonely, the oppressed - grant them comfort, healing, and peace.

We pray for [insert specific intentions here] - may they experience your love and mercy in a powerful way.

Transformation and Gratitude:

We surrender ourselves to your will, Lord. Transform our hearts and minds, making us instruments of your peace and love in the world.

We offer our deepest gratitude for the gift of your Son, Jesus Christ. May his sacrifice forever guide our steps and inspire us to live a life worthy of your love.

In Jesus' name we pray,

Amen.

Additional Notes:

•Feel free to personalize this prayer by adding your own specific petitions and words of gratitude.

- You can incorporate this prayer into your daily novena reflections or use it during a dedicated prayer time.

- Remember, intercessory prayer involves praying for the needs of others. Consider including those close to you, as well as current world events, in your petitions.

Day 2: Blood of Strength and Courage - Finding Fortitude in Christ

Exploring the Theme: Strength for Martyrs, Saints, and Everyday Believers

Today's reflection delves into the theme of strength and courage associated with the Precious Blood of Jesus Christ. We will explore how the sacrifice on the cross provides fortitude not only for martyrs and saints, but also for everyday believers like ourselves facing challenges in our daily lives.

Scripture Reading:

Today's scripture reading focuses on the story of Stephen, the first Christian martyr, found in Acts 7:54-60.

Reflection Points:

•As you read the passage, consider Stephen's unwavering faith even in the face of persecution.
•What gave him the strength to endure such suffering?

•Reflect on the concept of martyrdom. While martyrdom is often associated with dramatic acts of sacrifice, how can everyday acts of courage and faith be seen as a form of witnessing to Christ?

Strength for Everyday Believers:

•The challenges we face in daily life may not be as dramatic as those faced by martyrs, but they can still be daunting. Consider a situation in your own life where you need strength and courage.

•How can meditating on the sacrifice of Christ and the power of His Precious Blood provide you with the fortitude to persevere?

Inspirational Examples:

- Throughout history, countless saints have drawn strength from their faith. Think of a saint you admire for their courage and perseverance. What can you learn from their example?

- Consider people in your own life who demonstrate remarkable strength and resilience. How do they inspire you?

<u>Finding Fortitude in Christ:</u>

The Precious Blood of Christ is not just a symbol of sacrifice, but also a source of immense strength. How can reflecting on this concept bring you courage in your daily struggles?

What practical steps can you take to cultivate a deeper connection to the power of the Precious Blood in your life? Consider prayer, meditation, or seeking guidance from a spiritual leader.

Prayer:

Dear Lord,

As I reflect on the immense sacrifice of your Son, Jesus Christ, I am filled with awe and gratitude. His courage in the face of suffering inspires me.

Grant me the strength to overcome the challenges I face in my own life. Help me to find solace and fortitude in the power of Your Precious Blood.

May I, like the saints and martyrs, live a life that reflects your teachings and bears witness to your love.

In Jesus' name,

Amen.

Additional Thoughts:

Today's theme is particularly relevant for those facing difficult situations, illnesses, or personal struggles. Reflect on how the concept of strength and courage can be applied to your specific circumstances.

Consider incorporating inspirational stories of martyrs and saints into your daily reflections. There are many resources available online and in libraries that can provide uplifting examples of faith and perseverance.

Readings and Reflections - Examples of Strength Inspired by Christ's Blood

Scripture Reading: Acts 7:54-60 **(The Martyrdom of Stephen)**

Reflection:

Today's scripture reading narrates the story of Stephen, the first Christian martyr. Read the passage attentively, focusing on Stephen's unwavering faith even as he faces persecution and death.

• What words or actions from Stephen stand out to you?

• How does he demonstrate strength and courage in the face of his impending death?

Beyond Dramatic Martyrdom:

Martyrdom is often associated with dramatic sacrifices for faith. However, consider the concept of witnessing to Christ in everyday life:

Think of situations where you might need to stand up for your beliefs, even if it means facing disapproval or ridicule.

• How can small acts of courage, like defending someone being bullied or speaking out against injustice, be seen as forms of witnessing?

Strength in Daily Life:

We all face challenges in daily life, from overcoming bad habits to dealing with difficult relationships. Consider:

- What personal struggles are you currently facing?

- How can reflecting on the sacrifice of Christ and the power of His Precious Blood give you strength to persevere?

Seeking Inspiration from Saints:

Throughout history, countless saints have drawn immense strength from their faith. Research a saint known for their courage and resilience. Here are some examples:

> - Saint Joan of Arc: A young woman who led the French army in battle, inspired by her visions.

- Saint Maximilian Kolbe: A priest who volunteered to die in a concentration camp in place of a fellow prisoner.

- Saint Mother Teresa: Devoted her life to serving the poorest of the poor, overcoming immense challenges.

- What can you learn from these inspirational figures? How does their faith inspire your own?

Finding Strength in Christ:

Reflect on how meditating on the sacrifice of Christ and the power of His Precious Blood can provide strength in daily struggles. Here are some questions to consider:

- How does the concept of Christ's unwavering love and courage in the face of suffering inspire you?

- What are some practical ways you can cultivate a deeper connection to this power in your life? (e.g., prayer, meditation, scripture reading)

<u>Sharing Your Reflections:</u>

Consider journaling your thoughts and feelings after reading and reflecting.

Discussing these themes with a trusted friend or family member can deepen your understanding and provide mutual support.

Additional Resources:

- Numerous online resources and libraries offer biographies of saints and martyrs. Explore these stories to find examples that resonate with you.
- Consider reading books or articles about everyday heroes who have shown remarkable courage and resilience.

- Remember, the strength inspired by Christ's Blood is not reserved for the extraordinary. We can all find the courage to face challenges and live a life of faith in our daily experiences.

Day 2 – Novena to the Precious Blood of Jesus

Let us begin in the name of the Father, and of the Son, and of the Holy Spirit. Amen.

By the power of Thy Blood, O Jesus, I seek Thy assistance and implore Thy help in this time of need.

O Jesus, I kneel at Thy bleeding feet, pleading for Thy attention. Countless graces and mercies have been bestowed through Thy Blood. My hope endures in You until the end of my days.

O Jesus, through the Precious Blood shed for our souls, each drop poured out for our redemption, and the tears of Thy Immaculate Mother, I earnestly beseech Thee to hear my prayer:

(Mention your request here…)

O Jesus, throughout Thy mortal life, You consoled countless sufferers, healed numerous infirmities, and often uplifted the downtrodden; have mercy on my soul as it cries to Thee from the depths of anguish.

O Jesus, from the wounds of Thy heart, may a wave of Thy merciful Blood flow forth, granting me the grace I ardently desire.

O Jesus, hasten the moment when my tears will be transformed into joy and my sighs into thanksgivings.

Holy Mary, I ask for your intercession in seeking this aid. But above all, God our Father in heaven, "May Your will be done." Amen.

Recite: Our Father... Hail Mary... Glory Be...

Jesus, Crucified, Have Mercy on Me

Daily Prayer: Seeking Courage for Challenges and Spiritual Growth

Heavenly Father,

As we journey through this second day, we come before you with hearts open to your guidance and strength. We acknowledge the challenges that lie ahead, the obstacles that may test our faith and resolve.

Seeking Courage:

We confess moments of doubt and fear that may hold us back.

Embolden us with the courage to face difficulties with unwavering faith in your presence.

Grant us the strength to overcome adversity and emerge stronger in our walk with you.

Fueling Spiritual Growth:

We recognize that challenges are often catalysts for growth.

Open our eyes to the lessons hidden within each obstacle.

Guide us to learn from our experiences and deepen our reliance on your grace.

Drawing from Your Strength:

We remember the countless times you have delivered us from hardship.

Remind us of your unwavering love and unwavering presence in our lives.

Fill us with the courage of Christ, who faced his trials with unwavering faith and unwavering trust in your will.

Empowering Others:

Grant us the courage to stand beside others facing their own challenges.

Inspire us to offer words of comfort and acts of support, reflecting your love in the world.

Closing:

We place our trust in you, O Lord. May we walk through this day and beyond, empowered by your courage, fortified by your love, and ever-growing in our spiritual journey.

In Jesus' name, ***Amen.***

Reflection:

•Take a moment after the prayer to reflect on a specific challenge you are facing.

•How can you apply the themes of courage and spiritual growth to this situation?

•Write down your thoughts in a journal or simply hold them in your heart as you move forward.

Reflective Journaling: Identifying Areas Where You Need Strength

As we delve deeper into the novena dedicated to the Precious Blood of Jesus Christ, take some time for introspection and self-reflection. The concept of Christ's sacrifice is linked to immense strength and courage. Today's prompt invites you to explore areas in your life where you might need this kind of strength.

<u>Identifying Challenges:</u>

Current Struggles:

> Think about your current life situation. Are you facing any challenges that require strength and perseverance? This could be anything from overcoming a bad habit to dealing with a difficult relationship or work situation. Be honest with yourself and write down a few specific challenges you're currently encountering.

Fears and Anxieties:

We all have fears and anxieties that can hold us back. Reflect on your own fears. **Are there anxieties that prevent you from taking risks or pursuing your goals?** Write down a few specific fears or anxieties that might be hindering your growth.

Standing Up for Beliefs:

Consider situations where you might need the courage to stand up for what you believe in. This could involve defending someone from bullying, speaking out against injustice, or simply voicing your opinion when it's different from the majority. **Are there any situations where you might need strength to stand by your convictions?** Write down a few scenarios where you might need courage to act on your beliefs.

Seeking Strength from Christ:

Connecting to the Precious Blood:

> Reflect on how the concept of Christ's sacrifice and the shedding of His blood relates to the theme of strength and courage. **How can meditating on this concept provide you with the fortitude you need to face your challenges?** Write down your thoughts and feelings.

Finding Inspiration:

> Think of people in your life who demonstrate remarkable strength and resilience. These could be friends, family members, historical figures, or even characters from literature or movies. **How do they inspire you?** Write down the names of these individuals and a few qualities you admire about them.

Action Steps:

Based on your reflections, identify one specific area where you need more strength. **What small, practical step can you take today to begin cultivating more courage in this area?** Write down this action step as a commitment to yourself.

Remember:

There are no right or wrong answers in journaling. Be honest with yourself and explore your thoughts and feelings openly.

This journaling prompt is a starting point. Feel free to add additional questions or reflections that are relevant to your own experiences.

Rereading your journal entries throughout the novena can help you track your progress and gain deeper insights.

By engaging in honest self-reflection and connecting with the strength offered by the Precious Blood of Christ, you can begin to navigate your challenges with greater courage and resilience.

Litany of the Precious Blood

Lord, have mercy.

Christ, have mercy.

Lord, have mercy.

Precious Blood of Jesus Christ, save us. (repeated throughout)

Precious Blood of Jesus Christ, shed in the Garden of Gethsemane, save us. Precious Blood of Jesus Christ, flowing forth in the Scourging at the Pillar, save us. Precious Blood of Jesus Christ, crowning You with Thorns, save us. Precious Blood of Jesus Christ, poured out as You carried the Cross, save us. Precious Blood of Jesus Christ, welling forth from Your Sacred Hands and Feet on the Cross, save us. Precious Blood of Jesus Christ, issuing from Your Most Sacred Heart, save us. Precious Blood of Jesus Christ, price of our redemption, save us. Precious Blood of Jesus Christ, inexhaustible fount of mercy, save us. Precious Blood of Jesus Christ, our drink of salvation, save us. Precious Blood of Jesus Christ, our cleansing wash, save us. Precious Blood of Jesus Christ, our strengthening power, save us. Precious Blood of Jesus Christ, our eternal hope, save us.

Lamb of God, who takes away the sins of the world, spare us, O Lord. (repeated once)

Lamb of God, who takes away the sins of the world, graciously hear us, O Lord. (repeated once)

Lamb of God, who takes away the sins of the world, grant us peace, O Lord. (repeated once)

Leader: *Let us pray.*

Almighty and eternal God, we adore Your Son, our Lord Jesus Christ, who shed His Precious Blood for our redemption. Grant that we may ever cherish its benefits and through its power be brought to the eternal inheritance. Through the same Christ our Lord.

Response: *Amen.*

Day 3: Blood of Cleansing and Purification - Embracing the Power of Redemption

Scriptural Basis: The Blood as Cleansing Agent and Washing Away of Sins

Today's reflection focuses on the Precious Blood of Jesus Christ as a powerful symbol of cleansing and purification. Scripture offers numerous passages that connect blood with the concept of atonement and forgiveness. Through Christ's sacrifice, a path to redemption and a renewed relationship with God is made possible.

Scripture Reading:

Today's scripture reading is Leviticus 17:11, which states: **"For the life of the flesh is in the blood, and I have given it to you on the altar** to make atonement for yourselves. It is the blood that makes atonement for one's life." (Leviticus 17:11)

Reflection Points:

In the Old Testament, sacrificial offerings often involved the shedding of blood. Consider the concept of blood being linked to atonement in this passage. How does this foreshadow the significance of Christ's sacrifice in the New Testament?

Reflect on the concept of cleansing and purification. Think of how rituals of cleansing were practiced in ancient cultures. **How can the idea of Christ's blood washing away our sins be understood metaphorically?**

The Power of Redemption:

Redemption refers to the act of being saved from sin or captivity. How does the concept of Christ's sacrifice offer us the possibility of redemption?

Consider a time in your life when you felt the need for forgiveness or a fresh start. **How can reflecting on the power of Christ's blood bring a sense of peace and renewal?**

Finding Forgiveness and Transformation:

Forgiveness is a crucial aspect of the cleansing and purifying power of the Precious Blood. Think about areas in your life where you might need to forgive yourself or others. **How can the concept of Christ's sacrifice guide you towards forgiveness and reconciliation?**

Reflect on how the idea of being cleansed by Christ's blood can lead to personal transformation. **How can this concept inspire you to live a life that reflects God's love and grace?**

Prayer:

Dear Lord,

As I contemplate the immense sacrifice of your Son, Jesus Christ, I am filled with awe and gratitude. The shedding of His Precious Blood offers the promise of cleansing and redemption.

Wash away my sins, Lord. Grant me the grace to forgive myself and others. Open my heart to the transformative power of your love.

Guide me on a path of renewal, allowing me to live a life worthy of your sacrifice.

In Jesus' name,

Amen.

Additional Thoughts:

Today's theme is particularly relevant for those seeking forgiveness, healing, and a fresh start in their spiritual journey.

Consider incorporating activities that symbolize cleansing and purification into your novena experience. This could involve taking a long bath or spending time in nature.

Reflect on how you can share the message of forgiveness and redemption with others through your words and actions.

Guided Meditation: Visualizing Purification Through Christ's Sacrifice

Finding a Quiet Space:

Begin by creating a sacred space for your meditation. Find a quiet corner, perhaps light a candle, and silence any distractions. Take a few deep breaths to center yourself and open your heart to the experience.

Visualization: The Cleansing Light

•Imagine yourself standing in a peaceful place, perhaps a meadow bathed in warm sunlight. Feel the gentle breeze on your skin and the calmness of nature surrounding you.

•As you stand there, visualize a soft, white light emanating from above. This light represents the love and grace of God. Allow the light to envelop you completely, washing away any stress, anxiety, or negativity you may be carrying.

•Now, focus on an area of your life where you feel the need for cleansing or forgiveness. This could be a past mistake, a resentment you hold towards someone, or simply a general feeling of burden.

•See this burden as a dark stain on your clothing or aura. As the white light continues to bathe you, visualize the stain lifting and dissolving, carried away by the light.

The Sacrifice and the Blood

Now, shift your focus to the image of Jesus Christ on the cross. Acknowledge the pain and suffering he endured for your sake. See the blood flowing from his wounds.

•In your mind's eye, see this blood not as a symbol of violence, but as a powerful force of cleansing and redemption. Imagine the blood washing over the areas you identified as needing purification.

•Feel the stain dissolving completely, replaced by the pure white light of God's love and forgiveness.

Renewed and Cleansed

- Spend some time basking in this feeling of purification and renewal. Imagine yourself standing tall, free from burdens, and filled with the light of God's grace.

- See yourself moving forward in your life with a lighter heart and a renewed sense of purpose.

Bringing the Light into Your Life

- Slowly begin to bring your awareness back to the present moment. Take a few deep breaths and gently wiggle your fingers and toes.

- Carry the feeling of purification with you throughout your day. Remember the cleansing power of the Precious Blood and the transformative love of Christ.

Additional Tips:

If your mind wanders during the meditation, gently refocus on the visualization.

You can use calming music or guided meditation recordings to enhance your experience.

Feel free to adapt the visualization to fit your own beliefs and preferences.

This guided meditation is meant to be a starting point. The most important aspect is to approach it with an open mind and allow yourself to be guided by the spirit.

Day 3 – Novena to the Precious Blood of Jesus

Let us begin in the name of the Father, and of the Son, and of the Holy Spirit. Amen.

By the power of Thy Blood, O Jesus, I seek Thy assistance and implore Thy help in this time of need.

O Jesus, I kneel at Thy bleeding feet, pleading for Thy attention. Many graces and mercies have flowed from Thy Blood. My hope remains steadfast in You until the end of my days.

O Jesus, through the Precious Blood shed for our souls, each drop poured out for our redemption, and the tears of Thy Immaculate Mother, I earnestly beseech Thee to hear my prayer:

(Mention your request here…)

O Jesus, throughout Thy mortal life, You consoled countless sufferers, healed numerous infirmities, and often uplifted the downtrodden; have mercy on my soul as it cries to Thee from the depths of anguish.

O Jesus, from the wounds of Thy heart, may a wave of Thy merciful Blood flow forth, granting me the grace I ardently desire.

O Jesus, hasten the moment when my tears will be transformed into joy and my sighs into thanksgivings.

Holy Mary, I ask for your intercession in seeking this aid. But above all, God our Father in heaven, "May Your will be done." Amen.

Recite: Our Father... Hail Mary... Glory Be...

Jesus, Crucified, Have Mercy on Me

Prayer for Forgiveness and Renewal

Almighty God,

With a heart heavy with regret, I come before you seeking forgiveness. The weight of my transgressions burdens me, and I yearn for the cleansing power of your grace.

I acknowledge the hurt I have caused, both to myself and to others. My words and actions have strayed from your path, and I deeply regret the pain I have inflicted.

Open my heart to the truth, Lord. Grant me the strength to confront my shortcomings and take responsibility for my choices.

Through the sacrifice of your Son, Jesus Christ, a path to redemption is offered. His Precious Blood washes away sin and offers the promise of a fresh start.

I confess my sins, Lord, and surrender to your mercy. Cleanse me from all unrighteousness and renew my spirit with your love.

Guide me on a journey of forgiveness, both for myself and for those who have trespassed against me. May I extend the same compassion and understanding you have shown me.

Fill me with the strength to turn away from temptation and embrace a life that reflects your teachings. Empower me to live with a renewed sense of purpose, walking in the light of your love.

In Jesus' name,

Amen.

Self-Examination Prompts: Acknowledging Areas for Growth

Honest self-reflection is a crucial step in personal development. These prompts will guide you in exploring areas where you might need to focus your growth efforts.

Mindset and Habits:

Negative Self-Talk: Do you find yourself engaging in negative self-talk? How does this inner critic hold you back?

Procrastination: Do you struggle with procrastination? What are some underlying reasons for putting things off?

Unhealthy Habits: Are there any habits in your life (e.g., excessive screen time, unhealthy eating) that you'd like to change? What are the first steps you can take to address them?

Relationships and Communication:

Conflict Resolution: How do you handle conflict in your relationships? Are there areas where you could improve your communication skills?

Empathy and Compassion: Do you struggle to understand the perspectives of others? How can you cultivate more empathy and compassion in your interactions?

Unhealthy Relationships: Are there any relationships in your life that are draining or negative? How can you set healthy boundaries or remove yourself from these situations?

Values and Goals:

Living Your Values: Do your actions and choices reflect your core values? If not, how can you bridge the gap between your ideals and your behavior?

Setting Goals: Do you have clear goals for your personal and professional life? What steps can you take to make progress towards your aspirations?

Fear of Failure: Does the fear of failure hold you back from taking risks or pursuing your dreams? How can you cultivate a growth mindset and learn from setbacks?

Spiritual Growth:

Connecting with Something Larger: Do you feel a connection to something larger than yourself? This could be a spiritual connection, a sense of purpose, or a feeling of belonging to a community.

Regular Reflection: Do you make time for regular self-reflection and introspection? How can you incorporate practices like meditation or journaling into your routine?

Living Your Faith: If you identify with a particular faith tradition, how can you more actively integrate your beliefs into your daily life?

Remember:

•There are no right or wrong answers in self-examination. Be honest with yourself and explore your thoughts and feelings openly.

•This is just a starting point. Feel free to add additional prompts or areas for reflection that are relevant to your own life journey.

•Acknowledging areas for growth is the first step towards positive change. Once you identify areas that need improvement, you can begin to develop strategies for personal development.

•By engaging in regular self-reflection and taking action on your insights, you can cultivate a deeper understanding of yourself and unlock your full potential for growth.

86

Act of Consecration to the Precious Blood

Conscious and merciful Savior,

In humble recognition of my unworthiness and Your divine greatness, I prostrate myself at Your feet and express profound gratitude for the countless manifestations of Your grace bestowed upon me, Your undeserving servant. I am especially thankful for delivering me from the destructive clutches of Satan through Your Precious Blood.

In the presence of my beloved Mother Mary, my guardian angel, my patron saint, and the entire heavenly host, I willingly dedicate myself with a sincere heart, O dearest Jesus, to Your Precious Blood. Through this Blood, You have redeemed the world from sin, death, and damnation. With the assistance of Your grace and to the utmost of my abilities, I pledge to promote and cultivate devotion to Your Precious Blood, the ransom for our salvation, so that Your adorable Blood may be revered and glorified by all.

Thus, I seek to atone for my past indifference towards Your Precious Blood of love and to make amends for the many offenses committed by humanity against this invaluable price of our redemption. O that my own sins, apathy, and every act of disrespect towards You, O Holy Precious Blood, could be undone.

Behold, O dearest Jesus, I offer You the love, honor, and adoration which Your most Holy Mother, Your faithful disciples, and all the saints have rendered to Your Precious Blood. I implore You to pardon my past faithlessness and indifference, and to forgive all who offend You.

Bathe me, O Divine Savior, and all humanity, in Your Precious Blood, so that we, O Crucified

Love, may henceforth love You with all our hearts and duly honor the price of our salvation. Amen.

We seek refuge in your protection, O holy Mother of God; do not disregard our pleas in our times of need, but deliver us always from every danger, O glorious and blessed Virgin. Amen.

For All Benefactors of this Devotion:

Our Father... Hail Mary... Glory Be...

Blood of Jesus intoxicates me!

O Jesus, my Beloved Savior,

always present in the Tabernacle

to strengthen, rejoice, and nourish souls,

I come to dedicate myself to Your Precious Blood,

pledging You my sincere love and fidelity.

Moved to sorrow by the memory of Your sufferings,

the contemplation of the Cross,

and the thought of the insults

and contempt heaped upon Your dear Blood by ungrateful souls,

I yearn, O my Jesus,

to bring joy to Your Heart

and to make You forget my sins

and those of the whole world

by consecrating my body and soul to Your service.

*I desire, my Jesus, to live from now on
only by Your Blood and for Your Blood.
I choose It as my greatest treasure
and the dearest object of my love.*

*O merciful Redeemer,
please regard me as a perpetual worshipper
of Your Most Precious Blood,
and accept my prayers, deeds, and sacrifices
as acts of reparation and love.*

*Heavenly Wine,
source of purity and strength,
pour into my soul.
Make my heart a living chalice
from which grace shall continually flow
upon those who love You,
especially upon poor sinners who offend You.*

*Teach me to honor You
and to lead others to honor You.
Grant me the power to draw cold and hardened hearts to You,
so they may experience how infinitely
Your consolations surpass those of the world.*

*O Blood of my Crucified Savior,
detach me from the world and its spirit.
Make me love suffering and sacrifice,
following the example of St. Catherine of Siena,
who loved You so deeply
(and whom I choose again today as my special patroness).*

*O Precious Blood,
be my strength amidst the trials and challenges of life.
Grant that at the hour of death*

*I may bless You for having been the comfort
and sanctification of my soul,
before becoming, in Heaven,
the eternal object of my love and praise.*

*Saints of God,
who owe your happiness to the Blood of Jesus;
Angelic spirits,
who proclaim Its glory and power;
August Virgin,
who owe to It the privileges
of your Immaculate Conception
and Divine Maternity,
assist me in offering perpetual homage to the Precious Blood of my Redeemer
through adoration, reparation, and thanksgiving.*

Day 4: Blood of Unity and Reconciliation - Healing Brokenness and Building Bridges

Theme Exploration: The Blood as a Unifying Force, Mending Divisions

Today's reflection delves into the concept of the Precious Blood of Jesus Christ as a powerful force for unity and reconciliation. We explore how Christ's sacrifice offers the possibility of healing brokenness, mending divisions within ourselves and in the world around us.

Scripture Reading:

Today's scripture reading is Ephesians 2:13-18, which speaks of the unity brought about by

Christ's sacrifice: "**But now in Christ Jesus you who once were far off have become near by the blood of Christ. For he himself is our peace, who has made both one and has broken down in his flesh the dividing wall of hostility, by abolishing the law of commandments expressed in ordinances, so that he might create in himself one new man in place of the two, thus making peace, and might reconcile us both to God in one body through the cross, killing the hostility in his flesh.**" (Ephesians 2:13-18)

Reflection Points:

In the passage from Ephesians, Paul describes Christ's sacrifice as breaking down the dividing wall of hostility. Consider divisions that exist in the world today – social, political, religious. How can the message of unity through Christ's blood inspire us to bridge these divides?

•Reflect on areas of brokenness or conflict within yourself. Are there relationships that need mending? How can the concept of reconciliation through Christ's blood guide you towards forgiveness and healing?

The Power of Reconciliation:

Reconciliation is the process of restoring broken relationships or creating peace after a disagreement. **How can the concept of reconciliation inspire us to reach out to those we have disagreements with?**

Forgiveness is a crucial element of reconciliation. Think of someone you need to forgive. **How can reflecting on the immense forgiveness offered through Christ's sacrifice inspire you to forgive others?**

Building Bridges:

The concept of building bridges signifies creating connections across differences. Consider ways you can build bridges in your own life. This could involve reaching out to someone from a different background or simply being more understanding towards those with different viewpoints.

Prayer:

Dear Lord,

We reflect on the immense sacrifice of your Son, Jesus Christ, whose blood was shed to unite us all. We acknowledge the divisions that exist in our world, the walls of hostility that separate us from one another.

Grant us the courage to tear down these walls, Lord. Inspire us to reach out to those we disagree with, to bridge the gaps and build bridges of understanding and compassion.

Empower us with the spirit of forgiveness, allowing us to let go of resentment and embrace reconciliation. May the love poured out through Christ's sacrifice guide us towards a world united in peace and harmony.

In Jesus' name,

Amen.

Additional Thoughts:

Today's theme is particularly relevant for those who are involved in reconciliation efforts or working towards social justice.

Consider ways you can actively promote unity and understanding in your community. This could involve volunteering for organizations that bridge divides or simply having conversations with people from different backgrounds.

Remember, reconciliation is a process that takes time and effort. Be patient with yourself and others as you work towards healing and unity.

Scriptural Examples: Passages Highlighting Reconciliation Through Christ

Here are some powerful scripture examples that highlight reconciliation through Christ:

Ephesians 2:13-18: This passage, explored in Day 4, beautifully describes Christ as the bridge between humanity and God. It speaks of Him breaking down the "dividing wall of hostility" and creating "one new man" through His sacrifice. (Ephesians 2:13-18)

Colossians 1:19-22: This verse emphasizes the universality of reconciliation through Christ. It states that God was "**pleased to reconcile to himself all things through him, by making peace through the blood of his cross**." (Colossians 1:20)

Romans 5:10-11: This passage highlights reconciliation between humanity and God. Even though we were enemies of God, Christ's death reconciled us, allowing us to rejoice in God through Him. (Romans 5:10-11)

2 Corinthians 5:18-19: This verse emphasizes God's role in reconciliation. It states that God reconciled the world to Himself through Christ and gave us the "**ministry of reconciliation**." (2 Corinthians 5:18-19)

Matthew 5:23-24: This passage, while not directly mentioning Christ's blood, emphasizes the importance of reconciliation before offering sacrifices. Jesus instructs us to reconcile with anyone we have a grievance with before coming to the altar. (Matthew 5:23-24)

These are just a few examples, and the Bible offers many other verses that touch on the theme of reconciliation. Here are some additional pointers for finding relevant passages:

- **Search by keywords:** Use online Bible search tools and enter keywords like "reconciliation," "forgiveness," "unity," or "peace."
- **Focus on the New Testament:** The New Testament writings often emphasize the redemptive work of Christ, making them a rich source for finding relevant verses.
- **Explore specific books:** Consider books like Ephesians, Colossians, Romans, and Corinthians, as they frequently address themes of reconciliation and redemption.

By exploring these scriptures, you can gain a deeper understanding of the transformative power of Christ's sacrifice and its role in bringing about reconciliation between humanity and God, and among ourselves.

Day 4 – Novena to the Precious Blood of Jesus

Let us begin in the name of the Father, and of the Son, and of the Holy Spirit. Amen.

By the power of Thy Blood, O Jesus, I seek Thy assistance and implore Thy help in this time of need.

O Jesus, I kneel at Thy bleeding feet, pleading for Thy attention. Many graces and mercies have flowed from Thy Blood. My hope remains steadfast in You until the end of my days.

O Jesus, through the Precious Blood shed for our souls, each drop poured out for our redemption, and the tears of Thy Immaculate Mother, I earnestly beseech Thee to hear my prayer:

(Mention your request here…)

O Jesus, throughout Thy mortal life, You consoled countless sufferers, healed numerous infirmities, and often uplifted the downtrodden; have mercy on my soul as it cries to Thee from the depths of anguish.

O Jesus, from the wounds of Thy heart, may a wave of Thy merciful Blood flow forth, granting me the grace I ardently desire.

O Jesus, hasten the moment when my tears will be transformed into joy and my sighs into thanksgivings.

Holy Mary, I ask for your intercession in seeking this aid. But above all, God our Father in heaven, "May Your will be done." Amen.

Recite: Our Father... Hail Mary... Glory Be...

Jesus, Crucified, Have Mercy on Me

Daily Prayer for Peace and Healing in Relationships

Dear Lord,

As we journey through this novena dedicated to the Precious Blood of your Son, Jesus Christ, we come before you seeking peace and healing in our relationships.

We acknowledge the brokenness that exists in our connections with others, the misunderstandings, hurts, and walls that have been built over time. We recognize our own shortcomings and the ways we may have contributed to these strains.

Grant us the grace to forgive, Lord. Empower us to let go of resentment and embrace the transformative power of your love. Guide us towards reconciliation, even when it feels difficult or seems impossible.

Fill us with the courage to reach out, to mend what is broken, and to build bridges of understanding. Open our hearts to compassion and empathy, allowing us to see things from the perspectives of others.

May the sacrifice of your Son inspire us to act with love and kindness in all our interactions. Bless our relationships with renewed strength, trust, and forgiveness.

We pray for the healing of past hurts, the strengthening of present bonds, and the courage to build new connections rooted in love and respect.

In Jesus' name,

Amen.

Journaling Prompt: Identifying Broken Relationships

As we delve deeper into the concept of reconciliation through Christ's Precious Blood, take some time for introspection and self-reflection. This prompt invites you to explore areas in your life where relationships might be broken or in need of healing.

Identifying Brokenness:

Relationships in Need of Repair: Reflect on your current relationships (family, friends, romantic, work colleagues). Are there any relationships that feel strained, distant, or unresolved?

- Write down the names of individuals with whom you have a broken relationship.

- Briefly describe the nature of the strain or distance.

Your Role in the Brokenness: Consider your own contributions to the brokenness in these relationships.

- Were there any actions or words on your part that may have caused hurt or resentment?

- Be honest with yourself, but avoid self-blame.

The Desire for Reconciliation: Do you have a desire to mend these broken relationships? This doesn't necessarily mean becoming best friends again, but rather achieving a sense of peace and understanding.

- Write down your honest feelings about the possibility of reconciliation for each relationship.

The Power of Reconciliation:

Forgiveness as a Starting Point: Reflect on the concept of forgiveness as a crucial element of reconciliation. Is there anyone you need to forgive, or do you need to forgive yourself for something related to these broken relationships?

> •Write down the names of individuals you need to forgive, or acknowledge areas where self-forgiveness might be needed.

Seeking Guidance from Christ: Consider how the concept of Christ's sacrifice and the power of His blood can inspire you towards reconciliation. How can reflecting on this concept give you strength and courage to reach out and heal these broken bonds?

> •Write down your thoughts and feelings about seeking guidance from Christ in fostering reconciliation.

Taking the First Step: While reconciliation may be a long-term process, consider a small, practical step you can take today to initiate the healing process. This could be a simple act of reaching out, offering a sincere apology, or simply acknowledging the hurt that has occurred.

- Write down a specific action you can take towards reconciliation for each relationship, even if it's a small first step.

Remember:

There are no right or wrong answers in journaling. Be honest with yourself and explore your thoughts and feelings openly.

This prompt is a starting point. Feel free to add additional questions or reflections that are relevant to your own experiences.

Rereading your journal entry throughout the novena can help you track your progress and gain deeper insights.

By engaging in honest self-reflection and drawing inspiration from the power of reconciliation through Christ's sacrifice, you can begin to mend broken relationships and build bridges of understanding in your life.

Intercessory Prayer for Reconciliation in the Wider World

Almighty God,

We stand before you today, hearts heavy with the burdens of a divided world. Walls of suspicion and hatred separate nations, communities, and even families. Violence and conflict erupt, causing suffering and tearing at the fabric of society.

We reflect on the immeasurable sacrifice of your Son, Jesus Christ, whose Precious Blood symbolizes unity and reconciliation. His love transcended all boundaries, embracing humanity in its entirety.

We implore you, Lord, to break down the walls that divide us. Soften hearts hardened by prejudice and anger. Replace suspicion with understanding and hatred with compassion.

Guide the leaders of nations towards dialogue and peace. Inspire them to work together for the common good, prioritizing the well-being of all people.

Bless the peacemakers and those who work tirelessly to bridge divides. Empower them with courage and perseverance in their endeavors.

Grant us, your children, the strength to be agents of reconciliation in our own spheres of influence. May our words and actions promote understanding and respect for people of all backgrounds and beliefs.

Help us to see the common humanity that binds us all, children of the same God, yearning for peace and love.

May the power of Christ's Precious Blood wash away the stains of division and conflict, paving the way for a world united in harmony and peace.

In Jesus' name, ***Amen.***

111

Day 5: Blood of Compassion and Healing - Experiencing Divine Mercy

Examining the Theme: The Blood as a Source of God's Unconditional Love and Healing

Today's reflection focuses on the Precious Blood of Jesus Christ as a powerful symbol of God's unconditional love and healing mercy. Through Christ's sacrifice, we are offered not only forgiveness but also the potential for healing – physical, emotional, and spiritual.

Scripture Reading:

Today's scripture reading is Isaiah 53:4-5, which speaks of the healing power of the suffering servant: "**Surely he has borne our griefs and carried our sorrows; yet we esteemed him**

stricken, smitten by God, and afflicted. But he was wounded for our transgressions; he was crushed for our iniquities; upon him was the chastisement that brought us peace, and with his stripes we are healed." (Isaiah 53:4-5)

Reflection Points:

The passage from Isaiah describes the suffering servant as bearing our burdens and healing our wounds. Consider how the concept of Christ's sacrifice connects to the idea of God's healing power.

Reflect on areas in your life where you might need healing. This could be physical illness, emotional wounds, or spiritual struggles. **How can meditating on the sacrifice of Christ bring comfort and hope for healing?**

Experiencing Divine Mercy:

- Divine Mercy refers to God's boundless compassion and forgiveness. Consider how the concept of Christ's blood offering us redemption relates to the idea of Divine Mercy.

- Reflect on times in your life when you have experienced God's mercy. **How did this experience impact you?**

Seeking Healing:

While faith can be a powerful source of healing, it's important to acknowledge the importance of seeking professional help when needed. Consider different forms of healing, such as traditional medicine, therapy, or spiritual practices like prayer and meditation.

Prayer:

Dear Lord,

We come before you today, hearts filled with both gratitude and longing. We are grateful for the immense sacrifice of your Son, Jesus Christ, whose blood symbolizes your boundless love and healing mercy.

We acknowledge the pain and suffering present in our lives. We carry physical wounds, emotional burdens, and spiritual struggles. Open our hearts to the healing power of your love, Lord.

Grant us the strength to seek the help we need, be it through medicine, therapy, or the solace of prayer and community. Guide us on a path of healing, both physical and spiritual.

May the shedding of Christ's Precious Blood wash away our pain and fill us with your healing grace. Renew our hope and grant us the peace that surpasses all understanding.

In Jesus' name,

Amen.

Additional Thoughts:

Today's theme is particularly relevant for those who are struggling with illness, loss, or any form of suffering.

Consider incorporating practices like prayer, meditation, or spending time in nature as ways to connect with God's healing presence.

Remember, healing is often a journey, not a destination. Be patient with yourself and trust in God's love and mercy to guide you through the process.

Readings and Reflections: Miracles and Healing Through Christ's Blood

The concept of miracles and healing through Christ's blood is a powerful theme in Christianity. This reflection explores scriptural passages, theological interpretations, and personal reflections on this concept.

Scriptural Basis:

The Bible offers numerous passages that connect Jesus' ministry with acts of healing and miracles. Here are a few key examples:

Mark 1:40-45: This passage describes Jesus healing a leper, demonstrating his power over illness.

Matthew 8:5-13: Here, Jesus heals a centurion's servant, highlighting his willingness to heal even those outside his immediate community.

John 5:1-9: In this story, Jesus heals a paralyzed man at the Pool of Bethesda, signifying his power to heal on the Sabbath and his authority over illness.

These are just a few examples, and the Gospels contain many more accounts of Jesus' healing ministry. It's important to note that these passages are open to various interpretations. Some see them as literal miracles, while others understand them as symbolic representations of Jesus' power to bring wholeness and healing.

Theological Interpretations:

The concept of healing through Christ's blood has been interpreted in various ways throughout

Christian history. Here are two main perspectives:

Sacrificial Atonement: This view emphasizes Jesus' sacrifice on the cross as a form of payment for humanity's sins. His blood is seen as offering not just forgiveness but also the potential for healing, both physical and spiritual.

Symbol of Divine Love and Power: Another interpretation focuses on the blood as a symbol of God's boundless love and power. Jesus' willingness to shed his blood signifies God's desire to heal and restore humanity.

Personal Reflections:

How do these scriptural passages and theological interpretations resonate with your own faith?

Have you experienced healing in your life, either physical or emotional? If so, how did you connect this experience to your faith?

Do you believe in miracles of healing? Why or why not?

Additional Thoughts:

The concept of healing through Christ's blood can be a source of comfort and hope for those facing illness or struggling with other challenges.

•It's important to remember that faith is not a guarantee of physical healing. However, it can provide strength, peace, and a sense of connection to something larger than oneself during difficult times.

•If you are struggling with illness, consider seeking professional medical help alongside your spiritual practices.

Deepening Your Exploration:

•Research different Christian denominations' views on healing through Christ's blood.

•Read stories of people who have experienced faith-based healing.

•Reflect on how your faith can bring comfort and hope in times of suffering.

By engaging with scripture, theological interpretations, and personal reflection, you can gain a deeper understanding of the concept of miracles and healing through Christ's blood.

• Day 5 – Novena to the Precious Blood of Jesus

Let us begin in the name of the Father, and of the Son, and of the Holy Spirit. Amen.

By the power of Thy Blood, O Jesus, I seek Thy assistance and implore Thy help in this time of need.

O Jesus, I kneel at Thy bleeding feet, pleading for Thy attention. Many graces and mercies have flowed from Thy Blood. My hope remains steadfast in You until the end of my days.

O Jesus, through the Precious Blood shed for our souls, each drop poured out for our redemption, and the tears of Thy Immaculate Mother, I earnestly beseech Thee to hear my prayer:

(Mention your request here…)

O Jesus, throughout Thy mortal life, You consoled countless sufferers, healed numerous infirmities, and often uplifted the downtrodden; have mercy on my soul as it cries to Thee from the depths of anguish.

O Jesus, from the wounds of Thy heart, may a wave of Thy merciful Blood flow forth, granting me the grace I ardently desire.

O Jesus, hasten the moment when my tears will be transformed into joy and my sighs into thanksgivings.

Holy Mary, I ask for your intercession in seeking this aid. But above all, God our Father in heaven, "May Your will be done." Amen.

Recite: Our Father... Hail Mary... Glory Be...

Jesus, Crucified, Have Mercy on Me

Prayer for Healing (Physical, Emotional, Spiritual)

Almighty God,

I come before you today seeking your healing touch. I place before you the burdens I carry, both physical, emotional, and spiritual.

Physical Healing: *If I am experiencing illness or pain, I surrender my body to your care. Grant me the strength to endure and guide the hands of those who provide medical attention. (Mention specific ailments if comfortable)*

Emotional Healing: *If I am struggling with emotional wounds, anxieties, or fears, I open my heart to your comforting presence. Wash away my pain with your love and grant me the* *strength to move forward. (Mention specific emotions if comfortable)*

Spiritual Healing: *If I am feeling lost, disconnected, or burdened by sin, I seek your forgiveness and renewal. Guide me on a path of spiritual growth and lead me closer to you.*

Through the precious blood of your Son, Jesus Christ, I pray for healing. His sacrifice represents your boundless love and mercy. May his wounds become channels of grace, pouring forth your healing power into my life.

Grant me wisdom to discern the best path to healing, whether through medicine, therapy, or simply the solace of your presence. Surround me with your love and guide me towards wholeness.

In Jesus' name,

Amen.

Guided Visualization: Experiencing God's Healing Love

Finding a Quiet Space:

Begin by creating a sacred space for your meditation. Find a quiet corner, perhaps light a candle, and silence any distractions. Take a few deep breaths to center yourself and open your heart to the experience.

Visualization:

•Imagine yourself standing in a peaceful meadow bathed in warm sunlight. Feel the gentle breeze on your skin and the calmness of nature surrounding you.

•As you stand there, visualize a radiant light emanating from above. This light represents the love and healing power of God. Allow the light to envelop you completely, washing away any stress or negativity you may be carrying.

•Focus on the area of your life where you need healing. This could be a physical ailment, an emotional wound, or a spiritual struggle. See this area as a dark or cloudy spot within your being.

•Now, visualize the radiant light intensifying, focusing on the area that needs healing. See the darkness begin to dissolve, replaced by the warm, healing light of God's love.

•Feel the light filling you with a sense of peace and well-being. Imagine the pain or burden being carried away by the light, leaving behind a feeling of lightness and renewal.

Connecting with the Divine:

•In your mind's eye, see yourself reaching out towards the source of the light. Feel a sense of connection with the divine, with God's healing presence.

•If you have a prayer or specific request for healing, offer it now in your mind. You can silently express your needs or simply bask in the feeling of God's love and compassion.

Integrating the Healing:

- Spend some time basking in this feeling of healing and wholeness. Imagine yourself standing tall and radiant, filled with the light of God's love.

- See yourself carrying this feeling of healing with you throughout your day. Believe in your body's ability to heal, your mind's capacity for resilience, and your spirit's strength to overcome challenges.

Bringing the Light into Your Life:

- Slowly begin to bring your awareness back to the present moment. Take a few deep breaths and gently wiggle your fingers and toes.

Remember the feeling of peace and healing you experienced during the meditation. Carry this feeling with you throughout your day, allowing it to guide your thoughts and actions.

Additional Tips:

If your mind wanders during the meditation, gently refocus on the visualization.

You can use calming music or guided meditation recordings to enhance your experience.

Feel free to adapt the visualization to fit your own beliefs and preferences.

This guided meditation is meant to be a starting point. The most important aspect is to approach it with an open mind and allow yourself to be guided by the spirit.

Prayer for Those in Need of Healing

Almighty God,

With compassion and love, we lift up before you all those in need of your healing touch. We see the suffering:

The physically ill, those battling chronic pain or sudden injury. Grant them strength to endure, wisdom in seeking treatment, and the comfort of your presence. (Mention specific illnesses if appropriate)

The emotionally wounded, carrying burdens of grief, loss, anxiety, or depression. Soothe their hearts, mend their broken spirits, and surround them with your love. (Mention specific emotions if appropriate)

The spiritually lost, yearning for meaning and purpose. Guide them on a path of faith, open their hearts to your love, and grant them the strength to find peace within them.

We pray for the doctors, nurses, therapists, and caregivers who tirelessly work to bring healing to others. Empower them with skill, compassion, and knowledge. Guide their hands and bless their efforts.

For those who have lost hope, ignite a spark of faith within them. Remind them of your unwavering love and your promise of comfort in times of need.

Through the precious blood of your Son, Jesus Christ, we pray for healing. May his sacrifice be a beacon of hope, reminding us of your boundless love and mercy.

We surrender these needs to your care, O God. Work your miracles of healing, both physical and spiritual, in the lives of those who suffer.

In Jesus' name, **Amen.**

130

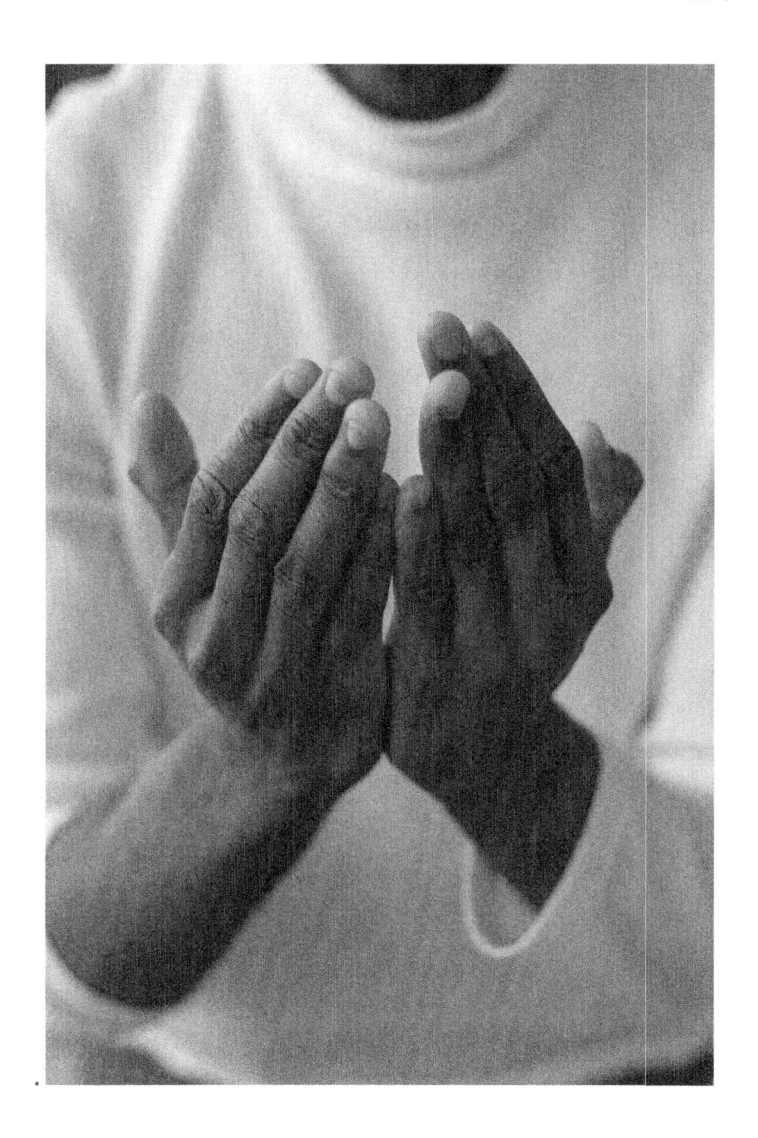

Day 6: Blood of Hope and New Life - Finding Transformation and Strength

Scriptural Exploration: The Blood as a Symbol of Resurrection and New Beginnings

Today's reflection delves into the concept of the Precious Blood of Jesus Christ as a symbol of hope, new life, and transformation. Through Christ's sacrifice and resurrection, we are offered the possibility of a renewed relationship with God and the strength to overcome challenges in our lives.

Scripture Reading:

Today's scripture reading is **Romans 6:3-4,** which speaks of the transformative power of Christ's death and resurrection: **"Do you not**

know that all of us who have been baptized into Christ Jesus were baptized into his death? We were buried therefore with him by baptism into death, so that as Christ was raised from the dead by the glory of the Father, we too might walk in newness of life." (Romans 6:3-4)

Reflection Points:

The passage from Romans describes baptism as being "**buried**" with Christ and rising with him in newness of life. Consider how the concept of Christ's blood offering forgiveness and redemption relates to the idea of starting anew.

Reflect on areas in your life where you might desire transformation. This could involve overcoming negative habits, pursuing a new path, or simply letting go of the past to embrace the future. **How can meditating on the sacrifice of Christ inspire you to seek positive change?**

Finding Hope and Strength:

Hope is the belief that things can improve and that the future holds promise. Strength is the capacity to face challenges and persevere through difficulties.

Consider how the concept of Christ's sacrifice offers hope and strength in the face of life's challenges. **How can reflecting on his blood spilled for humanity inspire you to overcome obstacles?**

Transformation Through Faith:

Transformation refers to a significant change in form, appearance, or character. Faith can be a powerful force for transformation, guiding us towards a more meaningful and fulfilling life.

Reflect on how your faith has transformed you or how you hope it will transform you in the future. **How can the concept of Christ's blood shed for you inspire you to become a better person?**

Prayer:

Dear Lord,

We come before you today, hearts filled with both gratitude and longing. We are grateful for the immense sacrifice of your Son, Jesus Christ, whose blood symbolizes hope for new life and the promise of transformation.

We acknowledge the areas in our lives that need change. We yearn to break free from negative patterns, overcome challenges, and embrace a renewed sense of purpose.

Grant us the strength to embark on this journey of transformation, Lord. Fill us with the hope that comes from knowing your love and forgiveness.

Empower us with the courage to face our fears and the perseverance to overcome obstacles. May the shedding of Christ's Precious Blood be a source of strength, reminding us that we are not alone on this path.

Guide us towards a life that reflects your love and grace. Transform us into the people you created us to be.

In Jesus' name,

Amen.

Additional Thoughts:

•Today's theme is particularly relevant for those seeking personal growth, overcoming addiction, or facing difficult life transitions.

•Consider incorporating practices like prayer, meditation, or spending time in nature to connect with the transformative power of faith.

•Remember, transformation is a journey, not a destination. Be patient with yourself and trust in God's grace to guide you on the path towards a renewed life.

Day 6 – Novena to the Precious Blood of Jesus

Let us begin in the name of the Father, and of the Son, and of the Holy Spirit. Amen.

By the power of Thy Blood, O Jesus, I seek Thy assistance and implore Thy help in this time of need.

O Jesus, I kneel at Thy bleeding feet, pleading for Thy attention. Many graces and mercies have flowed from Thy Blood. My hope remains steadfast in You until the end of my days.

O Jesus, through the Precious Blood shed for our souls, each drop poured out for our redemption, and the tears of Thy Immaculate Mother, I earnestly beseech Thee to hear my prayer:

(Mention your request here…)

O Jesus, throughout Thy mortal life, You consoled countless sufferers, healed numerous infirmities, and often uplifted the downtrodden; have mercy on my soul as it cries to Thee from the depths of anguish.

O Jesus, from the wounds of Thy heart, may a wave of Thy merciful Blood flow forth, granting me the grace I ardently desire.

O Jesus, hasten the moment when my tears will be transformed into joy and my sighs into thanksgivings.

Holy Mary, I ask for your intercession in seeking this aid. But above all, God our Father in heaven, "May Your will be done." Amen.

Recite: Our Father... Hail Mary... Glory Be...

Jesus, Crucified, Have Mercy on Me

Daily Prayer for Hope and Transformation

Almighty God,

As we journey through this novena, we stand before you today seeking hope and transformation. We acknowledge the limitations and struggles present in our lives. We yearn to break free from negativity, embrace new beginnings, and walk a path aligned with your will.

The sacrifice of your Son, Jesus Christ, fills us with hope. His blood shed for humanity signifies your boundless love and the promise of a transformed life. We draw strength from his resurrection, a testament to the power of overcoming darkness and death.

Grant us the courage to confront our shortcomings and the humility to seek forgiveness. Guide us towards releasing past burdens and embracing the potential for growth.

Fill our hearts with the unwavering hope that comes from faith in you. Remind us that with your love as our foundation, we can face any challenge and overcome any obstacle.

Empower us to take concrete steps towards the transformation we desire. Open our minds to new possibilities and guide us on the path towards becoming the best versions of ourselves.

May the precious blood of Christ be a constant source of strength and inspiration. May it remind us that we are not alone on this journey, but forever embraced by your love and grace.

In Jesus' name,

Amen.

Reflective Journaling: Identifying Areas for Personal Transformation

As we delve deeper into the concept of transformation through the Precious Blood, use this prompt to explore areas in your life where you might seek positive change. Remember, transformation is a journey, and honest self-reflection is the first step.

<u>Seeds of Change:</u>

Yearning for Transformation: Do you feel a desire for personal growth or a sense of needing to change certain aspects of your life? This might be related to habits, behaviors, or simply a desire for a more fulfilling life. Write down what initially comes to mind.

Areas for Improvement: Reflect on specific areas where you might seek change. This could be anything from overcoming negative habits or procrastination to developing greater patience or pursuing a long-held dream. Be honest with yourself, but avoid harsh self-criticism.

Consider different aspects of your life:

- Personal habits and behaviors

- Relationships with others

- Career or life goals

- Spiritual growth

Motivation for Change: What motivates you to seek transformation in these areas? Is it a desire for greater happiness, improved well-being, or a sense of living up to your full

potential? Write down your motivations for change.

Transformation Through Faith:

Connecting Faith and Change: How can your faith inspire you to pursue personal transformation? Consider how reflecting on Christ's sacrifice and the power of his blood can give you strength and hope on your journey. Write down your thoughts and feelings.

Faith as a Source of Strength: Think about times in your life when your faith has helped you overcome challenges or make positive changes. **How did your faith provide support and guidance?**

Transformation Through Grace: Remember that transformation is not solely about your own efforts but also about God's grace working in your life. **How can accepting God's grace empower you on your path of change?**

Taking Action:

Small Steps, Big Journey: Significant change often begins with small, concrete steps. For each area you identified for improvement, consider a single, achievable action you can take in the next week. Write down these initial steps.

Seeking Support: Do you have a support system of friends, family, or a faith community that can encourage you on your journey? Who can you turn to for accountability and inspiration?

Remember:

There are no right or wrong answers in journaling. Be honest and open with yourself about your desires and challenges.

This is just a starting point. Feel free to add additional questions or reflections that resonate with you.

Rereading your journal entry throughout the novena can help you track your progress and gain deeper insights.

By engaging in honest self-reflection and drawing inspiration from the transformative power of Christ's sacrifice, you can set the stage for a journey of personal growth and become the best version of yourself.

Meditation on the Power of the Blood to Grant New Life

Finding a Quiet Space:

Begin by creating a peaceful environment for your meditation. Find a comfortable position, sitting or lying down, and take a few deep breaths to center yourself. If helpful, you can light a candle or play calming music.

Visualization:

Imagine yourself standing at the threshold of a darkened room. This room represents the limitations and burdens you carry within yourself. It could symbolize negative habits, past hurts, or a sense of stagnation.

As you stand there, a faint light appears in the distance. This light represents the hope of transformation and new life offered through Christ's sacrifice.

Focus on the light, and see it growing brighter and brighter. Feel a sense of curiosity and hope drawing you towards it.

Slowly, begin to step into the room. As you enter, notice the darkness begin to recede, pushed back by the radiant light. This light represents the power of Christ's blood, washing away negativity and offering the possibility of renewal.

See yourself walking further into the room, bathed in the warm, healing light. Imagine the light filling you from within, cleansing and purifying your spirit.

In your mind's eye, see any burdens or negativity you carry starting to dissolve in the

light. It could be a physical ailment, an emotional wound, or a limiting belief.

Focus on the feeling of lightness and renewal spreading through you. Feel yourself becoming energized and empowered by the transforming power of the light.

Connecting with the Divine:

Within the radiant light, see a gentle, loving presence. This presence represents the divine, God's love and grace surrounding you.

Silently offer a prayer of gratitude for the sacrifice of Christ and the hope of new life it offers.

If you have specific areas in your life where you desire transformation, focus on them in the light. Ask for God's guidance and strength to overcome challenges and embrace positive change.

Integrating the Light:

Spend some time basking in the feeling of peace, hope, and renewal. Imagine yourself carrying this light with you as you step back out of the darkened room.

See yourself returning to the present moment, feeling lighter and more energized. Know that the transformative power of the light remains within you.

Bringing the Light into Your Life:

Slowly begin to bring your awareness back to the present moment. Take a few deep breaths and gently wiggle your fingers and toes.

Remember the feeling of hope and renewal you experienced during the meditation. Carry this feeling with you throughout your day, allowing it to guide your thoughts and actions.

Additional Tips:

If your mind wanders during the meditation, gently refocus on the visualization.

You can use guided meditation recordings with visualizations related to transformation and new life.

Feel free to adapt the visualization to fit your own beliefs and preferences.

This meditation is meant to be a starting point. The most important aspect is to approach it with an open mind and allow yourself to be guided by the spirit.

Intercessory Prayer for Those Struggling with Loss or Despair

Almighty God, our hearts ache for those who walk in darkness, burdened by loss and despair.

We lift up before you all those facing the sting of grief, the crushing weight of disappointment, and the suffocating grip of hopelessness. May your presence, a beacon of love and compassion, illuminate their path.

For those grappling with the loss of loved ones, grant them solace in the knowledge that you are ever near. Ease their pain, mend their broken hearts, and replace their emptiness with the comforting warmth of your love.

For those drowning in despair, overwhelmed by life's hardships, ignite a spark of hope within them. Remind them of your unwavering love and your promise to see them through their darkest nights. Offer them strength to rise above their circumstances and find the will to carry on.

For those teetering on the edge of despair, contemplating paths of self-harm or destruction, surround them with your protective embrace. Show them a way forward, a reason to hold on. Guide them towards support and resources, and fill them with the knowledge that they are not alone.

Grant them, O God, the courage to face their pain, the strength to seek help, and the faith to believe in brighter days ahead.

May they, like seeds buried in darkness, find the light within themselves and blossom into renewed hope and joy.

Through the precious blood of your Son, Jesus Christ, who suffered and sacrificed for our redemption, we pray for healing, comfort, and a renewed sense of purpose for all who struggle.

In Jesus' name, ***Amen.***

Day 7: Blood of Light and Illumination - Finding Clarity and Direction

Today's reflection delves into the concept of the Precious Blood of Jesus Christ as a source of spiritual light and guidance. Through Christ's sacrifice, we are offered not only forgiveness but also the potential for illumination, helping us navigate life's challenges and find our path forward.

Examining the Theme: The Blood as a Source of Spiritual Light and Guidance

Scriptural Basis: We can find connections between light and God's guidance throughout the Bible. Psalms 119:105 (**"Your word is a lamp to my feet and a light to my path"**) and John 8:12 **("I am the light of the world. Whoever**

follows me will never walk in darkness but will have the light of life") establish this connection. While these verses don't directly mention blood, they connect light with God's presence and guidance.

Theological Interpretations: There are various ways to understand Christ's blood as a source of spiritual light and guidance:

> **Sacrificial Atonement:** This view emphasizes Jesus' sacrifice as a payment for humanity's sins. His blood is seen as illuminating the path to salvation and offering forgiveness, allowing us to walk in the light of God's grace.
>
> **Transformation and Illumination:** Another interpretation focuses on the transformative power of Christ's blood. By shedding his blood, Jesus is seen as offering us the opportunity to be cleansed and renewed, allowing us to see the world and ourselves with greater clarity.

Following Christ's Example: Some Christians see Christ's blood as a symbol of his teachings and the path he laid out. Following his teachings is seen as following the light, leading to a more meaningful and fulfilling life.

Personal Applications:

•**Reflect:** How does the concept of Christ's blood as a source of light and guidance resonate with your faith?

•**Seeking Guidance:** Do you actively seek spiritual guidance in your daily life? If so, how can reflecting on Christ's sacrifice inspire your decision-making?

•**Connecting with the Light:** Consider incorporating practices like prayer, scripture reading, spending time in nature, or meditation to connect with God's guiding light.

Additional Thoughts:

This theme offers comfort and hope. Even in darkness, God's light is present.

Spiritual guidance can come in many forms – prayer, scripture, wise counsel, or even moments of reflection.

Deepening Your Exploration:

Research: Explore writings of theologians who delve into the concept of Christ's blood as a source of light and guidance.

Reflection: Reflect on times in your life when you felt a sense of spiritual clarity or guidance. What role did your faith play?

Practices: Consider incorporating practices like contemplative prayer or journaling to seek spiritual guidance and discernment.

By engaging with scripture, theological interpretations, and personal reflection, you can gain a deeper understanding of Christ's blood as a source of spiritual light and guidance. This understanding can illuminate your path and inspire you to live a more meaningful life.

Prayer for Clarity and Direction:

Dear Lord,

As we conclude this novena dedicated to the Precious Blood, we stand before you seeking clarity and direction. The world can be a confusing place, and we often find ourselves unsure of the path to take.

We draw inspiration from the sacrifice of your Son, Jesus Christ. His blood, shed for humanity, illuminates the path towards you. We pray for the wisdom to discern your will in our lives.

Grant us the discernment to see opportunities where we might have seen obstacles. Open our hearts to the guidance you offer through prayer, scripture, and the wisdom of others.

Lead us away from darkness and confusion and towards the light of your love. May your will be our guide, and may your grace illuminate the path ahead.

In Jesus' name,

Amen.

Readings and Reflections: Passages Where Christ Offers Guidance and Wisdom

The teachings of Jesus Christ are a cornerstone of Christianity, offering timeless wisdom and guidance for navigating life's complexities. This exploration delves into scripture passages where Jesus imparts valuable lessons on various aspects of life.

The Gospels as a Guide:

The four Gospels (**Matthew, Mark, Luke, and John**) document the life, teachings, and ministry of Jesus Christ. These texts are rich with parables, sermons, and interactions with his disciples, offering a wealth of practical and spiritual wisdom.

Key Passages:

Here are a few prominent examples where Jesus offers guidance and wisdom:

The Sermon on the Mount (Matthew 5-7): This extended discourse covers a wide range of topics, including forgiveness, righteousness, prayer, and judging others. Jesus emphasizes humility, compassion, and living a life aligned with God's will.

The Great Commandment (Matthew 22:36-40): Jesus identifies the two most important commandments: loving God with all your heart, soul, and mind, and loving your neighbor as yourself. These principles serve as a foundation for ethical behavior and building strong relationships.

The Parable of the Prodigal Son (Luke 15:11-32): This story explores themes of forgiveness, unconditional love, and repentance. It reminds us of God's boundless mercy and the importance of extending forgiveness to others.

The Golden Rule (Matthew 7:12): This simple yet profound statement captures the essence of ethical behavior: "Do unto others as you would have them do unto you." It encourages us to treat others with respect and compassion.

Reflection Points:

Choose one of the passages mentioned above or find another scripture where Jesus offers guidance that resonates with you. Read the passage slowly and reflect on its meaning.

Consider how the passage applies to your own life. **Are there areas where you can integrate Jesus' teachings into your thoughts, words, and actions?**

Discuss these passages with others. Sharing your reflections and insights can deepen your understanding and inspire others.

Additional Wisdom Teachings:

Jesus' teachings extend beyond specific passages. Here are some broader themes to explore:

Importance of Love: Love for God and love for others is a central theme in Jesus' teachings. Consider how to cultivate love in your daily interactions.

Forgiveness and Compassion: Jesus emphasizes forgiveness and compassion, even towards those who have wronged us. Reflect on how to practice these qualities in your life.

Humility and Service: Jesus teaches that true greatness comes from humility and serving others. Consider ways to incorporate service into your life.

Remember:

The teachings of Jesus are not meant to be a burden but rather a guide towards a more meaningful and fulfilling life. By actively engaging with scripture, reflecting on its meaning, and striving to integrate these principles into your daily life, you can experience the transformative power of Jesus' wisdom.

Day 7 – Novena to the Precious Blood of Jesus

Let us begin in the name of the Father, and of the Son, and of the Holy Spirit. Amen.

By the power of Thy Blood, O Jesus, I seek Thy assistance and implore Thy help in this time of need.

O Jesus, I kneel at Thy bleeding feet, pleading for Thy attention. Many graces and mercies have flowed from Thy Blood. My hope remains steadfast in You until the end of my days.

O Jesus, through the Precious Blood shed for our souls, each drop poured out for our redemption, and the tears of Thy Immaculate Mother, I earnestly beseech Thee to hear my prayer:

(Mention your request here…)

O Jesus, throughout Thy mortal life, You consoled countless sufferers, healed numerous infirmities, and often uplifted the downtrodden; have mercy on my soul as it cries to Thee from the depths of anguish.

O Jesus, from the wounds of Thy heart, may a wave of Thy merciful Blood flow forth, granting me the grace I ardently desire.

O Jesus, hasten the moment when my tears will be transformed into joy and my sighs into thanksgivings.

Holy Mary, I ask for your intercession in seeking this aid. But above all, God our Father in heaven, "May Your will be done." Amen.

Recite: Our Father... Hail Mary... Glory Be...

Jesus, Crucified, Have Mercy on Me

Prayer for Discernment and Clarity

Almighty God,

I stand before you today seeking clarity and guidance. The path ahead seems shrouded in uncertainty, and I yearn for the wisdom to make the right decisions.

Grant me, O Lord, the discernment to see opportunities where I might have seen obstacles. Open my heart and mind to the subtle nudges of your spirit, guiding me towards your will.

Bless me with the ability to sift through the noise and confusion of the world and hear your voice above all others. Silence the doubts and anxieties that cloud my judgment, and replace them with the unwavering light of your truth.

I place my trust in you, Lord. Lead me away from paths that lead astray and towards the direction that aligns with your purpose for my life. Equip me with the courage to take the next step, even if it feels uncertain, knowing that you walk beside me.

May your wisdom be my compass and your love the fuel that propels me forward.

In Jesus' name,

Amen.

Journaling Prompt: Identifying Areas Where You Seek Direction

Sometimes life throws us curveballs, leaving us feeling lost or unsure of the next step. This journaling prompt aims to help you identify areas in your life where you might be seeking direction from a higher power or your inner wisdom.

Step 1: Setting the Stage

- Begin by finding a quiet space and taking a few deep breaths to center yourself.
- Light a candle or play calming music if that helps create a reflective atmosphere.

Step 2: Identifying Areas of Uncertainty

•Imagine yourself standing at a crossroads. This crossroads represents the different paths or decisions you are facing in life.

Write down the different areas of your life where you feel uncertain or lack clear direction. This could include:

　•Career choices or job dissatisfaction

　•Relationship challenges or decisions

　•Personal growth or a desire for change

　•Spiritual development or a yearning for deeper meaning

　•Any other area where you feel lost or unsure

Step 3: Exploring Your Desires

For each area of uncertainty you identified, delve deeper.

What is your ideal outcome in this area? What would bring you a sense of fulfillment or purpose?

Write down your desires and aspirations for each aspect of your life.

Step 4: Seeking Guidance

- Reflect on how your faith or spirituality can guide you in these uncertain times.

- Can you think of any scripture passages, teachings, or personal experiences that offer wisdom or inspiration?

- Write down any insights or guiding principles that come to mind.

Step 5: Taking Action

Sometimes, even small steps can move you forward. For each area of uncertainty, brainstorm one or two concrete actions you can take in the next week to gain more clarity or move in a positive direction.

- Write down these actionable steps.

Closing Reflection:

After completing this journaling exercise, take a moment to reread what you have written.

Has this process helped you gain any new insights or a sense of direction?

Remember, this is just a starting point. Continue to reflect, pray, and seek guidance as you navigate these areas of uncertainty.

Additional Tips:

Be honest and open with yourself in your writing.

Don't be afraid to ask for help from trusted friends, mentors, or spiritual advisors.

There may not always be clear-cut answers. Trust that even in uncertainty, you are on the right path.

Act of Trust in the Guidance of the Holy Spirit

The Act of Trust in the Guidance of the Holy Spirit is a personal act of faith and surrender. Here are a few ways you can express this trust:

Prayer:

A heartfelt prayer is a powerful way to express your trust in the Holy Spirit. You can acknowledge your uncertainties and anxieties, and then ask the Holy Spirit to guide your thoughts, words, and actions.

Here's an example prayer:

Dear Holy Spirit,

I come before you today feeling lost and unsure. There are many decisions swirling in my mind, and I don't know which path to take. I surrender my anxieties and confusion to you. Guide my steps, illuminate the right path, and open my heart to receive your wisdom. Grant me the courage to trust your guidance, even when it feels uncertain.

In Jesus' name, ***Amen.***

Meditation:

Quieting your mind through meditation can create space for the Holy Spirit's voice to be heard. Focus on your breath, letting go of distracting thoughts. As you become calmer, ask the Holy Spirit to guide your intuition and inner wisdom.

Scripture Reading and Reflection:

Reading scripture with the intention of seeking guidance is another way to connect with the Holy Spirit. Choose a passage or book of the Bible that resonates with your current situation. Read slowly and reflect on the verses. Ask yourself how they might apply to your life and what message the Holy Spirit might be trying to convey.

Active Discernment:

Discernment is the ability to recognize the promptings of the Holy Spirit. Pay attention to your thoughts, feelings, and intuition. Does a certain course of action feel peaceful and right? •Are you experiencing a sense of joy or excitement about a particular decision? These can be signs that the Holy Spirit is guiding you.

Openness to Signs:

The Holy Spirit may guide you through **subtle signs**. Be open to synchronicities, recurring messages, or unexpected encounters that might nudge you in a certain direction. These signs can serve as confirmations of your intuition or a gentle nudge from the Holy Spirit.

Remember:

Trusting the Holy Spirit is a journey, not a destination. There will be times of uncertainty, but by actively seeking guidance through prayer, reflection, and discernment, you can cultivate a deeper connection with

the Holy Spirit and grow in your faith.

Day 8: Blood of Intercession and Advocacy - Finding Strength in Prayer

Understanding the Power of Intercessory Prayer

Today's reflection explores the concept of the Precious Blood of Jesus Christ as a source of strength in prayer, particularly through intercessory prayer. Through Christ's sacrifice, we are not alone in our struggles. We can approach God with confidence, knowing that his love extends to all, and that he hears our prayers for ourselves and others.

Understanding Intercessory Prayer:

Intercessory prayer is the act of praying on behalf of another person or cause. It's a form of advocacy, where we come before God and intercede for the needs of others.

Scriptural Basis:

The Bible offers numerous examples of intercessory prayer:

Abraham interceding for Sodom and Gomorrah (Genesis 18)

Moses interceding for the Israelites (Exodus 32)

Jesus interceding for his disciples (John 17)

These examples highlight the power of intercessory prayer and God's compassion for those in need.

The Power of Christ's Blood:

The blood of Christ is often seen as a symbol of his sacrifice and the bridge between humanity and God. His sacrifice is seen as offering forgiveness, reconciliation, and a pathway to a closer relationship with God.

How Christ's Blood Empowers Prayer:

Confidence in Approaching God: Because of Christ's sacrifice, we can approach God's throne with confidence, knowing that we are not condemned by our sins. (Hebrews 4:16)

Strength and Encouragement: Knowing that Jesus intercedes for us before the Father (Romans 8:34) provides strength and encouragement in our prayers.

Love and Compassion: Reflecting on Christ's sacrificial love can inspire us to pray with greater compassion for the needs of others.

Finding Strength in Intercessory Prayer:

Pray for Others: Consider the people in your life who are facing challenges. Lift them up in prayer, asking God for his love, grace, and intervention in their lives.

Become an Advocate: Is there a cause you feel passionate about? Pray for those affected and advocate for positive change.

Experience the Power of Unity: Praying for others, especially as part of a community, can be a powerful experience. Knowing you're not alone in lifting someone up strengthens your prayer.

Additional Thoughts:

Intercessory prayer is not about manipulating God's will, but about aligning our hearts with his love and compassion for all creation.

As you pray for others, remember to also pray for yourself. Seek God's guidance and strength in your own life.

Deepening Your Exploration:

•Research writings on the power of intercessory prayer and the role of the Holy Spirit in intercession.

•Reflect on times in your life when intercessory prayer has made a difference for you or someone you know.

•Consider incorporating regular intercessory prayer into your daily prayer routine.

- By understanding the power of Christ's sacrifice and the concept of intercessory prayer, you can experience a deeper sense of connection with God and find strength in lifting up the needs of others.

Scriptural Examples: Christ's Intercession for Humanity

The Bible offers several powerful examples of Christ's intercession for humanity, highlighting his ongoing role as advocate and mediator between God and humanity. Here are a few key passages:

Romans 8:34: "Who is to condemn? It is Christ Jesus, who died, yes, rather who was raised from the dead, who is at the right hand of God, who indeed is interceding for us." (NIV) This verse explicitly states that Christ actively intercedes for us before God the Father. His death and resurrection are seen as the ultimate act of intercession, offering us forgiveness and reconciliation.

Hebrews 4:14-16: "Since then we have a great high priest who has passed through the heavens, Jesus the Son of God, let us hold fast our confession. For we do not have a high priest who is unable to sympathize with our weaknesses, but one who in every respect has been tempted as we are, yet without sin. Let us then with confidence draw near to the throne of grace, that we may receive mercy and find grace to help in time of need." (NIV) This passage describes Jesus as our high priest, interceding on our behalf and offering us access to God's grace and mercy. His own experience with temptation allows him to understand our struggles and advocate for us with compassion.

John 17:9-11: "I am praying for them. I am not praying for the world, but for those whom you have given me, for they are yours. All mine are yours, and yours are mine, and I am

glorified in them. I do not ask that you take them out of the world, but that you keep them from the evil one." (NIV) In this passage, Jesus prays specifically for his disciples, but his intercession extends to all believers. He prays for their protection from evil and for their growth in faith.

1 Timothy 2:5-6: "For there is one God, and there is one mediator between God and men, the man Christ Jesus, who gave himself as a ransom for all, which is the testimony in its proper time." (NIV) This verse emphasizes the uniqueness of Christ's role as mediator. His sacrifice is seen as a ransom paid for all humanity, allowing us to be reconciled to God.

These are just a few examples, and the concept of Christ's intercession is woven throughout the

New Testament. By reflecting on these scriptures, we gain a deeper understanding of Christ's ongoing love and advocacy for us.

Day 8 – Novena to the Precious Blood of Jesus

Let us begin in the name of the Father, and of the Son, and of the Holy Spirit. Amen.

By the power of Thy Blood, O Jesus, I seek Thy assistance and implore Thy help in this time of need.

O Jesus, I kneel at Thy bleeding feet, pleading for Thy attention. Many graces and mercies have flowed from Thy Blood. My hope remains steadfast in You until the end of my days.

O Jesus, through the Precious Blood shed for our souls, each drop poured out for our redemption, and the tears of Thy Immaculate Mother, I earnestly beseech Thee to hear my prayer:

(Mention your request here…)

O Jesus, throughout Thy mortal life, You consoled countless sufferers, healed numerous infirmities, and often uplifted the downtrodden; have mercy on my soul as it cries to Thee from the depths of anguish.

O Jesus, from the wounds of Thy heart, may a wave of Thy merciful Blood flow forth, granting me the grace I ardently desire.

O Jesus, hasten the moment when my tears will be transformed into joy and my sighs into thanksgivings.

Holy Mary, I ask for your intercession in seeking this aid. But above all, God our Father in heaven, "May Your will be done." Amen.

Recite: Our Father... Hail Mary... Glory Be...

Jesus, Crucified, Have Mercy on Me

Prayer for the Needs of the Church and the World

Almighty God, we lift up before you the needs of your Church and the world.

For the Church:

Grant us wisdom and discernment to navigate the challenges we face. (Insert specific challenges your church or denomination faces)

Rekindle the flame of faith within our hearts and communities.

Ignite a passion for sharing your Gospel with love and compassion.

Foster unity within your Church, breaking down walls and building bridges of understanding.

Guide our leaders with your wisdom and empower them to shepherd your flock with love and integrity.

For the World:

We pray for those suffering from war, violence, and oppression. (Mention specific areas of conflict if you wish)

Grant comfort and healing to those who are sick, injured, or facing loss.

Guide the world's leaders towards wisdom, justice, and peace.

Open hearts to compassion and understanding, breaking down barriers of prejudice and hate.

Inspire acts of generosity and service to those in need.

For All:

May your love be a beacon of hope, illuminating the path forward in times of darkness.

Empower us to be instruments of your peace and love in the world.

Grant us the courage to stand up for what is right and defend the vulnerable.

Guide us to live according to your teachings, spreading kindness and love in all we do.

We pray in the name of Jesus Christ, your Son, our Lord and Savior.

Amen.

Chaplet of the Precious Blood

The Chaplet of the Precious Blood is a Catholic devotion used to honor the sacrifice of Jesus Christ and to petition God for various graces. Here's a breakdown of the Chaplet:

Materials:

A chaplet with five large beads and 50 small beads, or you can use a rosary.

A crucifix.

Opening Prayers:

Sign of the Cross: "In the name of the Father, and of the Son, and of the Holy Spirit. Amen"

Our Father (1x)

3 Hail Marys (3x)

Glory Be (3x)

Body of the Chaplet:

On each large bead:

Pray: "O most Precious Blood of Jesus Christ, heal the wounds of the whole world."

On each small bead:

Pray: "Eternal Father, I offer Thee the Most Precious Blood of Jesus Christ, in atonement for my sins and the sins of the whole world."

Closing Prayers:

Hail Holy Queen (1x)

Sign of the Cross: "May the Passion of our Lord Jesus Christ set a seal upon my heart, my mind, my memory, and all my faculties, both now and at the hour of my death. Amen"

Variations:

Some versions include an "Invocation of the Holy Spirit" before the Our Father.

You can find versions with additional prayers or meditations incorporated after the closing prayers.

<u>Here are some resources where you can learn more about the Chaplet of the Precious Blood:</u>

Church of the Transfiguration - Singapore

Precious Blood International

Intercessory Prayer for Specific Needs

Here's a powerful structure you can use to craft an intercessory prayer for specific needs:

1. Begin with Centering and Gratitude:

Take a few deep breaths to quiet your mind and center yourself in prayer.

Briefly express gratitude to God for your blessings and for the opportunity to intercede on behalf of others.

Example:

Dear Heavenly Father,

I come before you today in a spirit of gratitude for your love and presence in my life. Thank you for the many blessings I receive, and for the opportunity to lift up the needs of others in prayer.

2. Acknowledge the Specific Needs:

Clearly state the specific needs of the person(s) or situation you are praying for. Be specific and heartfelt in your request.

You can mention their name or situation directly.

Example:

Lord, I lift up to you [name of person] who is facing [specific challenge]. They are feeling [emotions they might be experiencing].

3. Petition God's Intervention:

Ask God to intervene in the situation according to His will.

You can pray for healing, guidance, strength, comfort, or any other specific need.

Example:

Grant them, O God, the strength to overcome this challenge. Guide them with your wisdom and fill them with your unwavering love.

4. Pray for Hope and Encouragement:

Ask God to offer hope and encouragement to the person(s) in need.

Example:

May they experience your unfailing love and find hope in your promises.

5. Conclude with Faith and Trust:

Close your prayer with an expression of faith and trust in God's power and love.

Example:

I place my trust in you, Lord, knowing that you are ever-present and always working for the good of those who love you.

In Jesus' name,

Amen.

Additional Tips:

•Personalize the prayer with your own words and feelings.

- Feel free to adapt the structure to fit the specific situation.

- You can pray silently or aloud.

- If you're praying for a group of people, you can mention them collectively or pray for them individually.

By following this structure and adding your own heartfelt petitions, you can create a powerful intercessory prayer for the specific needs you hold dear.

188

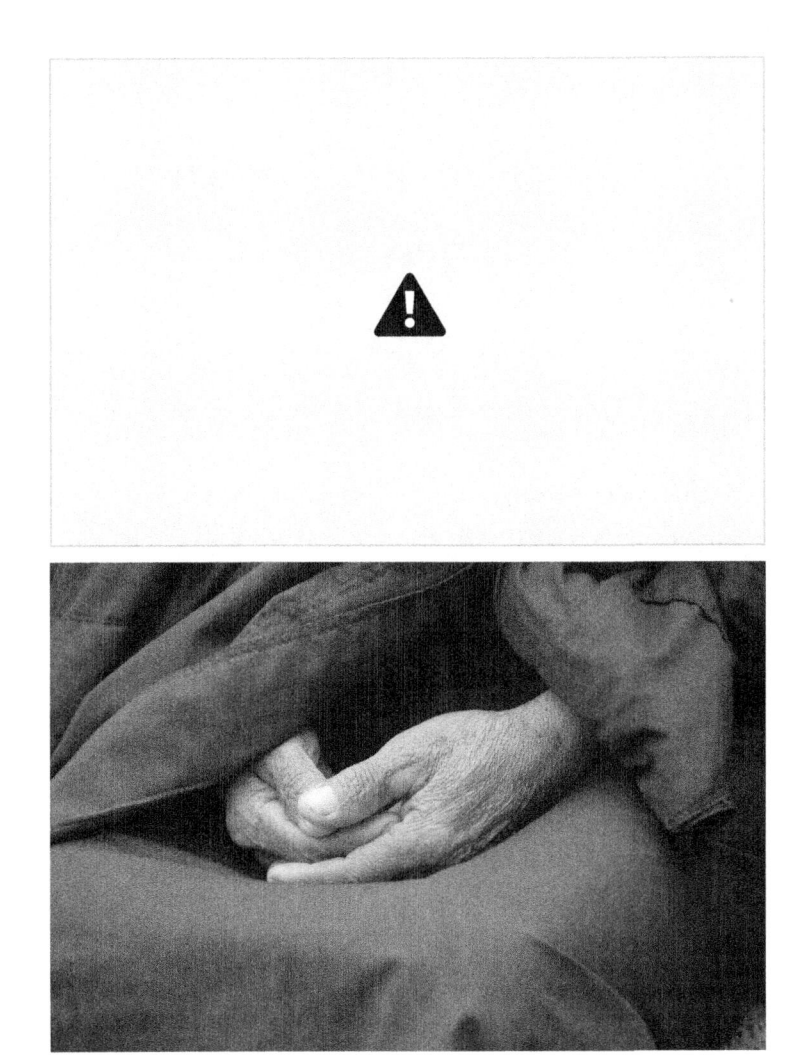

Day 9: Blood of Eternal Life - Gratitude and Looking Forward

Scripture Readings: Focus on Eternal Life Promised Through Christ's Sacrifice

Today's reflection focuses on the concept of the Precious Blood of Jesus Christ as a source of eternal life. Through his sacrifice, we are offered not only forgiveness but also the promise of everlasting life in communion with God.

Scripture Readings:

Here are a few key passages that highlight the promise of eternal life through Christ's sacrifice:

John 3:16: "For God so loved the world, that he gave his only Son, that whoever believes in him should not perish but have eternal life."

(NIV) This verse is a cornerstone of Christian belief, emphasizing God's love and the path to eternal life through faith in Jesus Christ.

John 14:6: **"Jesus answered, 'I am the way and the truth and the life. No one comes to the Father except through me.'"** **(NIV)** This verse emphasizes Jesus' central role in salvation and eternal life. He is the bridge between humanity and God.

Romans 6:23: **"For the wages of sin is death, but the free gift of God is eternal life in Christ Jesus our Lord."** **(NIV)** This verse contrasts the consequence of sin (death) with the gift of eternal life offered by God through Christ.

1 John 5:13: **"I write these things to you who believe in the name of the Son of God, that you may know that you have eternal life."**

(NIV) This verse offers assurance to believers, reminding them that faith in Jesus grants the gift of eternal life.

Reflecting on the Promise

Gratitude: Reflect on the profound gift of eternal life offered through Christ's sacrifice. Express gratitude for this transformative gift.

Hope: Allow the promise of eternal life to fill you with hope. Imagine the joy and peace that await you in communion with God.

Transformation: Consider how the promise of eternal life can inspire you to live a more meaningful life here on earth. Knowing your life has eternal significance can motivate you to use your time and talents wisely.

Looking Forward:

Living with Purpose: While eternal life awaits, we are called to live a purposeful life here on earth. Consider how your faith can guide your actions and inspire you to make a positive impact on the world.

Sharing the Promise: The promise of eternal life is a gift meant to be shared. Reflect on ways you can share your faith and the hope of eternal life with others.

Additional Thoughts:

The concept of eternal life is a mystery, but it offers a sense of hope and comfort, especially in the face of death and loss.

Focusing on the promise of eternal life does not diminish the importance of living a meaningful life here on earth.

Deepening Your Exploration

- Research writings on the concept of eternal life and its implications for Christian living.

- Reflect on your own beliefs about the afterlife. Does the concept of eternal life bring you comfort and hope?

- Discuss these themes with others and explore their perspectives on eternal life.

By reflecting on scripture, the promise of eternal life, and its implications for your life here on earth, you can cultivate a deeper sense of gratitude, hope, and purpose in your faith journey.

Day 9 – Novena to the Precious Blood of Jesus

Let us begin in the name of the Father, and of the Son, and of the Holy Spirit. Amen.

By the power of Thy Blood, O Jesus, I seek Thy assistance and implore Thy help in this time of need.

O Jesus, I kneel at Thy bleeding feet, pleading for Thy attention. Many graces and mercies have flowed from Thy Blood. My hope remains steadfast in You until the end of my days.

O Jesus, through the Precious Blood shed for our souls, each drop poured out for our redemption, and the tears of Thy Immaculate Mother, I earnestly beseech Thee to hear my prayer:

(Mention your request here…)

O Jesus, throughout Thy mortal life, You consoled countless sufferers, healed numerous infirmities, and often uplifted the downtrodden; have mercy on my soul as it cries to Thee from the depths of anguish.

O Jesus, from the wounds of Thy heart, may a wave of Thy merciful Blood flow forth, granting me the grace I ardently desire.

O Jesus, hasten the moment when my tears will be transformed into joy and my sighs into thanksgivings.

Holy Mary, I ask for your intercession in seeking this aid. But above all, God our Father in heaven, "May Your will be done." Amen.

Recite: Our Father... Hail Mary... Glory Be...

Jesus, Crucified, Have Mercy on Me

Closing Prayer of the Novena: Expressing Gratitude and Continued Commitment

Dear Heavenly Father,

As we conclude this Novena dedicated to the Precious Blood of your Son, Jesus Christ, we stand before you with hearts full of gratitude. Thank you for the countless blessings bestowed upon us, and for the profound gift of salvation offered through Christ's sacrifice.

Throughout these nine days of reflection, we have delved into the power of Christ's Blood – a symbol of sacrifice, forgiveness, redemption, guidance, intercession, and eternal life. We are forever grateful for the transformative impact of his love on our lives.

We acknowledge that this Novena marks an ending, but also a beginning. We commit to carrying the lessons learned and the inspiration received into our daily lives. May the lingering presence of Christ's Blood continue to:

Wash away our sins and guide us towards righteousness.

Offer us strength and courage in times of difficulty.

Illuminate the path ahead and grant us wisdom in our decisions.

Inspire us to be instruments of your love and compassion in the world.

Fill us with unwavering hope in the promise of eternal life.

Thank you for your unwavering love and presence in our lives. May we continue to grow in faith, hope, and love, forever grateful for the gift of your Son, Jesus Christ.

In Jesus' name,

Amen.

Reflective Journaling: Reflecting on Your Novena Experience and Commitments Moving Forward

Welcome!

As you conclude your Novena dedicated to the Precious Blood of Christ, this journaling prompt invites you to reflect on your experience and solidify the commitments you'd like to make moving forward.

Part 1: Reflecting on the Journey

Key Takeaways: What were some of the most powerful or meaningful insights you gained during this Novena?

Connecting Scriptures: Were there any particular scripture passages that resonated with you? Jot them down and ponder why they stood out.

Shifting Perspectives: Did this Novena cause any shifts in your perspective on the Precious Blood of Christ or your faith in general?

Challenges Faced: Did you encounter any challenges during your Novena journey? How did you navigate them?

Part 2: Commitments Moving Forward

Maintaining Focus: How can you integrate the lessons learned from this Novena into your daily life?

Actionable Steps: Identify 1-2 concrete actions you can take in the next week to keep the spirit of the Novena alive.

Deepening Your Faith: Are there any areas where you'd like to learn more about the Precious Blood or your faith in general?

Sharing the Message: Consider how you might share the message of hope and redemption found in Christ's sacrifice with others.

Prayer and Reflection: How can you incorporate prayer and reflection on the Precious Blood into your ongoing spiritual practice?

Remember:

• Be honest and open with yourself in your writing.

• Don't be afraid to revisit these reflections in the future and adapt your commitments as needed.

• A Novena is a springboard for ongoing spiritual growth. Use the momentum gained to keep moving forward in your faith journey.

Additional Tips:

- Spend some time in quiet prayer before beginning your journaling.
- Light a candle or play calming music to create a reflective atmosphere.
- Feel free to decorate your journal entries with colors, symbols, or drawings that resonate with you.

This journaling exercise is a personal exploration. Let your reflections guide you as you continue on your faith journey.

Litany of Thanksgiving to the Precious Blood

Here is a possible Litany of Thanksgiving to the Precious Blood:

Leader: Lord, have mercy.

Response: Lord, have mercy.

Leader: Christ, have mercy.

Response: Christ, have mercy.

Leader: Lord, have mercy.

Response: Lord, have mercy.

Leader: For the precious Blood shed for us at your Incarnation, we thank you, O Lord.

Response: We thank you, O Lord.

Leader: For the precious Blood shed for us in your Circumcision, we thank you, O Lord.

Response: We thank you, O Lord.

Leader: For the precious Blood shed for us in your Agony in the Garden, we thank you, O Lord.

Response: We thank you, O Lord.

Leader: For the precious Blood shed for us during your Scourging at the Pillar, we thank you, O Lord.

Response: We thank you, O Lord.

Leader: For the precious Blood shed for us during your Crowning with Thorns, we thank you, O Lord.

Response: We thank you, O Lord.

Leader: For the precious Blood shed for us as you carried the Cross, we thank you, O Lord.

Response: We thank you, O Lord.

Leader: For the precious Blood shed for us during your Crucifixion, we thank you, O Lord.

Response: We thank you, O Lord.

Leader: For the precious Blood and Water that flowed from your Sacred Heart, we thank you, O Lord.

Response: We thank you, O Lord.

Leader: For the precious Blood shed for us by your Five Holy Wounds, we thank you, O Lord.

Response: We thank you, O Lord.

Leader: For the precious Blood, the source of our redemption, we thank you, O Lord.

Response: We thank you, O Lord.

Leader: For the precious Blood, the life of the world, we thank you, O Lord.

Response: *We thank you, O Lord.*

Leader: *For the precious Blood, our drink of salvation, we thank you, O Lord.*

Response: *We thank you, O Lord.*

Leader: *For the precious Blood, our cleansing wash, we thank you, O Lord.*

Response: *We thank you, O Lord.*

Leader: *For the precious Blood, our strengthening power, we thank you, O Lord.*

Response: *We thank you, O Lord.*

Leader: *For the precious Blood, our eternal hope, we thank you, O Lord.*

Response: *We thank you, O Lord.*

Leader: *Lamb of God, you take away the sins of the world, have mercy on us.*

Response: *Lamb of God, you take away the sins of the world, have mercy on us.*

Leader: *Lamb of God, you take away the sins of the world, grant us peace.*

204

Response: *Lamb of God, you take away the sins of the world, grant us peace.*

Leader: *Let us pray.*

Almighty and eternal God, we give you thanks for the most precious Blood of your Son, our Lord Jesus Christ, shed for our redemption. Grant that we may ever cherish its benefits and through its power be brought to the eternal inheritance. Through the same Christ our Lord.

Response: *Amen.*

Appendix

Additional Prayers and Devotions Associated with the Precious Blood

Here are some additional prayers and devotions associated with the Precious Blood of Jesus Christ:

Prayers:

Anima Christi (Soul of Christ): This prayer reflects on the wounds of Christ and the power of his blood.

Prayer of Saint Bernard: This prayer expresses devotion to the Sacred Heart of Jesus and the Precious Blood.

Consecration to the Precious Blood: This prayer is a formal act of dedication to Jesus Christ through his Precious Blood.

Devotions:

The Holy Hour: This devotion involves spending an hour in prayer and reflection, often before the Blessed Sacrament. It can be dedicated to meditating on the sacrifice of Christ and the Precious Blood.

Eucharistic Adoration: Spending time in silent adoration before the Blessed Sacrament is a powerful way to connect with Jesus' presence and reflect on his sacrifice.

Feast of the Precious Blood: Celebrated on the first Friday after the Feast of Corpus Christi (Body of Christ), this feast specifically honors the Precious Blood of Jesus.

The Association of the Precious Blood: This Catholic organization promotes devotion to the

Precious Blood through various resources and activities. https://www.pbmr.org/

Additional Resources:

Books: Many books explore the theology and devotion to the Precious Blood. You can find recommendations from your local Catholic bookstore or library.

Websites: Several Catholic websites offer information and prayers related to the Precious Blood. You can search for reputable sources based on your denomination.

Important Note:

These are just a few examples, and the specific prayers and devotions associated with the Precious Blood may vary depending on your religious tradition and personal preferences. It's always wise to consult with your religious leader for guidance.

Resources for Further Study on the Theology of the Precious Blood

Here are some resources for further study on the theology of the Precious Blood of Jesus Christ:

Catholic Resources:

Websites:

> The Association of the Precious Blood: https://www.pbmr.org/
>
> **Catholic Answers:**
> https://www.catholic.com/encyclopedia/precious-blood

Franciscan Media:
https://www.franciscanmedia.org/ask-a-franciscan/eucharist-symbol-or-reality/

Books:

"The Precious Blood: A Theology of Salvation" by Michael J. O'Brien

"Power in the Blood" by Mark Miravalle

"United with Christ in the Eucharist: The Mystery of the Precious Blood" by Albert G. Ferrara

General Christian Resources:

Websites:

Christianity Today:
https://www.christianitytoday.com/ct/2006/may/9.29.html

Got Questions: https://www.gotquestions.org/blood-of-Christ.html

Books:

"The Blood of the Lamb" by John Piper

"The Power of the Blood" by Charles Stanley

Academic Resources:

Journals:

Theological Studies

The Catholic Theological Bulletin

Journal of Biblical Theology

Online Databases:

JSTOR (may require institutional access)

Academia.edu

ResearchGate (may require registration)

Remember:

As you explore these resources, be mindful of the specific denomination or tradition you are interested in, as their perspectives on the Precious Blood may differ.

It's always a good idea to consult with trusted religious leaders or scholars for guidance in your studies.

Consider attending lectures, workshops, or conferences related to the Precious Blood if available in your area.

I hope this helps!

Augustine Teresa

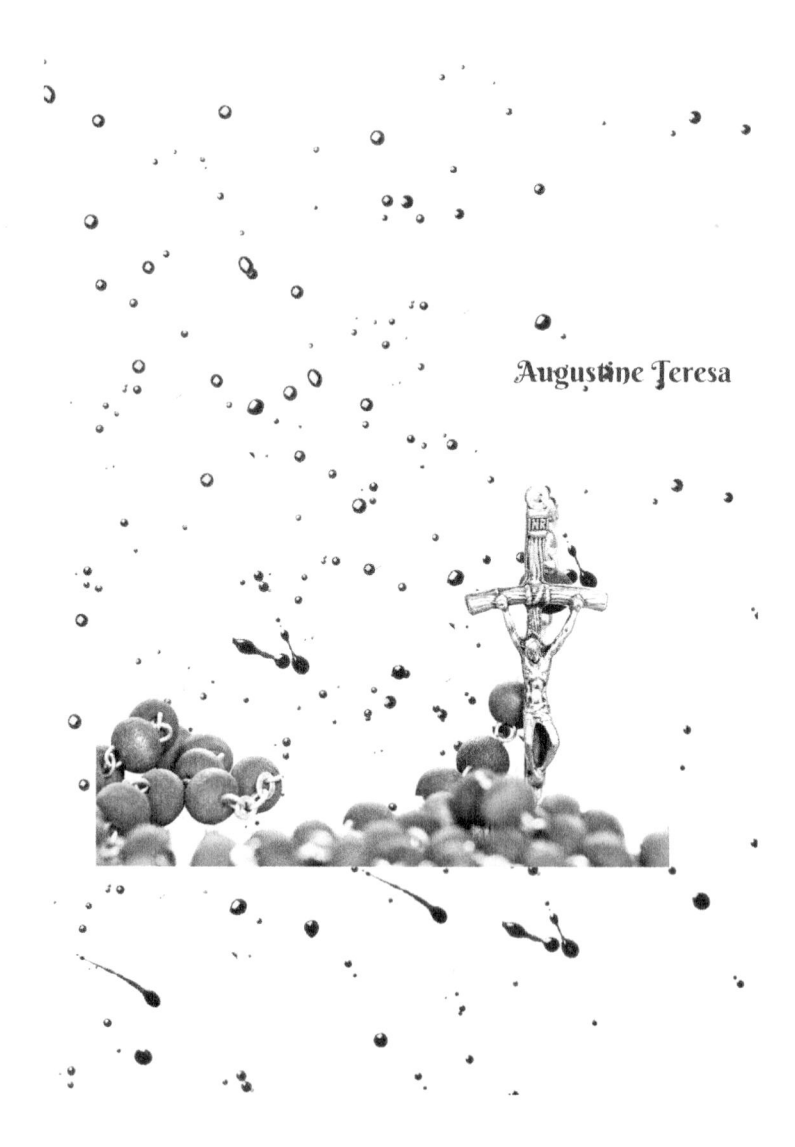

Printed in Great Britain
by Amazon